Agreed!
Improve Your Powers of Influence

Terry Gillen

INSTITUTE OF PERSONNEL AND DEVELOPMENT

Typesetting by Wyvern 21, Bristol
and printed in Great Britain by
the Cromwell Press, Trowbridge, Wiltshire

British Library Cataloguing in Publication Data
A catalogue record for this book is available from the
British Library

ISBN 0-85292-801-7

The views expressed in this book are the author's own
and may not necessarily reflect those of the IPD.

IPD House, Camp Road, Wimbledon, London SW19 4UX
Tel: 020-8971-9000 Fax: 020-8263-3333
Registered office as above. Registered Charity No. 1038333
A company limited by guarantee. Registered in England No. 2931892

Contents

Preface: influencing skills and the game of snooker   vii

Introduction   xi

1   Fundamental principles   1

2   Core skill one: persuasive probing   16

3   Core skill two: being assertive   43

4   Core skill three: building rapport   64

5   Core skill four: influencing groups   83

6   Understanding body language   89

7   Gameplans   102

8   Implementation   148

Index   154

Preface
influencing skills and the game of snooker

Here is a question for you. What do a fast-food restaurant manager, a consultant gynaecologist and a young public relations executive have in common? The answer is that they all attended one of my Positive Influencing Skills courses. They all shared a need to work more effectively with other people and, despite their undoubted *technical* competence, they were still learning *interpersonal* competence. No one had ever shown them how to *use* their behaviour *deliberately*. Their behaviour just happened. And sometimes behaviour just happens to be wrong!

I come across people, for example, who:

- need the co-operation of someone else, yet they use their behaviour to antagonise them
- want to change some aspect of a colleague or loved one, yet they use their behaviour to entrench the aspect still further
- need someone's agreement, yet they use their behaviour to cause the other person to disagree.

Behaviour is the link between what we want and what we get. Unfortunately, it is the link that is all too often neglected. It is a bit like when you are learning to play pool or snooker. Most people focus on the balls when they would do better to focus on their arms. After all, whether or not the balls go in the pockets is simply confirmation that you have done the correct thing with your arm. You will play better, therefore, if you focus first on getting your arm right and then on getting the balls in the pockets. This concept transfers readily to our behaviour both inside and outside work.

There is a growing need for influencing. Despite our intense use of modern technology, what we achieve has never been so dependent on our ability to influence others and to do so positively. At work, as the communication rules of the old 'command and control' structures wither, people's ability to get things done depends less on their position in the hierarchy and more on their influencing skills. Shop-floor workers are attending meetings, agreeing production schedules and contributing to quality procedures. Specialists, such as finance and marketing people, are having to persuade line colleagues of the value they bring, or face being one of the many functions outsourced in the next shake-out. In our personal lives, relationships that were once clear-cut and taken for granted are now subject to new pressures and require both new thinking and new skills to be maintained.

Yet most of us have in-built obstacles to performing better in face-to-face situations. Most of us behave by habit and, when those habits do not work, we rarely think of changing them. This is a pity because whenever I am coaching people I find myself highlighting the same problems time and time again – and guiding them through the same few core skills that would make an immense difference to what they achieve.

I also find that if guidance is to be beneficial, it has to pass the TSR Test. TSR stands for *That Sounds Reasonable*. I have learned that if my suggestions – whatever their psychological origins – do not have the ring of common sense, they are rarely accepted. Even if they are 'accepted' at the time, they are unlikely to make the eventual journey from classroom to workplace. If, on the other hand, they do sound reasonable, they are much more likely to be implemented.

This book concentrates on improving your face-to-face effectiveness with others. The intention is to help you use your behaviour to link the results you want in face-to-face situations with the results you get.

Like every other trainer I know, I have, over the years, soaked up a lot of information from conversations, books, articles and many other sources. Sometimes the origins of that information are well known but at other times they are way beyond my recollection. Wherever possible, therefore, when describing other people's work, I have made the appropriate acknowledgement. Should any information have slipped through the net, the lapse was entirely inadvertent.

Having said that, everything in this book has been tried and tested over a number of years on a variety of people, such as managers, professionals, specialists, bankers, scientists and engineers, male and female, young and not so young, etc. Those people have come from a variety of organisations, public and private, large and small, and from many different walks of life. Everything in this book has passed their TSR Test, as well as my own. The feedback I have received shows that it does make a difference both to people's influencing skills and to the quality and productivity of the relationships they enjoy in both their personal and professional lives. There is no doubt in my mind that the messages in this book will do the same for you. Whether or not they improve your snooker is more open to question.

June 1999

Introduction

Does this sound like you?

- Do you sometimes feel that people are being deliberately obstinate, slow or stupid?
- Do you ever find it odd that people cannot see the sense of what you are saying?
- Are there times when you just don't understand 'where the other person is coming from'?
- Is your behaviour often more of a response to your emotions rather than a considered action leading towards a positive outcome?
- Are there times when you are pushed, coerced, flattered or tricked into doing something you would rather not?

The ability to influence people, and to do so positively, is something that most of us could do better – and we should be all the better for it. Generally, *positive influencing* is not something that has been encouraged in us. (Even professional influencers, such as salespeople, do not always do it positively.) Yet it is a skill that enables us to achieve more when working with other people and it boosts our personal credibility. So what is it? How can you benefit from it? And why is it so important? Let's start by looking at how people react to social revolutions.

Revolution? ... What revolution?

Quite simply, the world in which most of us grew up is changing. At work, the drive for efficiency and global competitiveness has caused many organisations, large, small, public and private, to adopt concepts such as customer care, total quality, de-layering, matrix teams, re-engineering, empowerment, extensive use of IT and so on. These changes share two common features, First, they change the way we interact together. Second, they require skills different from those we needed to be successful in the past. Together, they amount to a revolution in relationships.

The past model of successful organisations is being replaced with a new model of success. The old one was characterised by large enterprises, tall hierarchies, superior and omnipotent management and an alienated workforce. The new one is characterised by small units, flat hierarchies, open, informal and participative team leadership and an involved workforce. The workforce has to be involved because, with modern business initiatives, success is just as dependent on a delivery van driver or a telephone sales clerk as it is on a senior manager.

This commercial reality is changing the way people at work relate to one another. In the old-model organisation, managers needed skills enabling them to command and control, to motivate, make decisions and solve problems etc, because these activities were their sole preserve.

Workers needed technical skills. In the new-model organisation, however, everybody needs skills to enable them to work as a team, to solve problems and to make decisions jointly, to be creative and, above all, to communicate.

And outside work?

Outside work, there are more 'joint breadwinner' couples, more intense use of leisure time for some and enforced leisure time for others, more homeworking, more self-employment and so on. This all puts pressure on our ability to interact with others if our relationships are to remain secure and invigorating.

These changes are so significant that the history books will probably regard them as revolutionary. One of the problems with social revolutions, however, is that they are easier to spot with hindsight than when you are actually living through them. The bottom line is that communication skills are fundamental to our personal effectiveness. So fundamental that the sooner you learn them the better. (We ought to teach them at school. After all, I do not know of a single relationship that faltered because one of the partners did not know the significance of the 1832 Reform Act or the major exports of Bolivia. But I know of plenty of relationship problems caused by poor-quality communication.)

True, I have presented this information in terms of extremes but I have done so to emphasise certain points. First, successful organisations now and in the future do not look like successful organisations of the past. Second, to be successful in them, you need to be able to interact successfully with others. The skills are exactly the same as those you need outside work to interact successfully with people in your personal life.

What's in it for me?

By learning positive influencing skills, you will achieve more of what you need in both your professional and personal life. You will do so with less time, less effort and less stress. Your personal credibility will go up. Relationships will be stronger. And, as an added bonus, you will be nicer to deal with.

What are *positive* influencing skills?

They are non-manipulative, persuading behaviours that demonstrate that you are treating people openly, honestly and respectfully. They enable you to achieve more with other people in such a way that people feel good about interacting with you.

But why *influencing* skills?

You may be asking yourself, 'Why influencing skills? Why not just face-to-face skills in general?' There are two reasons. First, most of us feel comfortable when information is neatly pigeon-holed. We tend to do the same with skills. We shall readily relate to selling skills, selection skills, appraisal skills, counselling skills, negotiating skills, and so on. In my experience as a skills trainer, however, there are only a few face-to-face skills – we simply use them in different ways in different situations. So it is more learning-efficient, and less repetitive, if we concentrate on acquiring the skills rather than on the situations in which we use them. Second, whether you are appraising, coaching, reprimanding or counselling, or just trying to get on with someone, you are in effect influencing. You are attempting to alter someone else's perceptions, views, beliefs, attitudes, decisions etc. Influencing skills form a common theme throughout most face-to-face situations.

1

Fundamental principles

The ideas you will learn from this book are based on certain beliefs about what constitutes effective influencing. So before we look at the skills we need to look at those beliefs to ensure that you and I are on the same wavelength and so appreciate the reasoning behind the skills I am advocating. These beliefs are so central to influencing skills I call them fundamental principles. In overview, they are:

- *Manipulative influencing has disadvantages for you.* While it might get you what you want in the short term, in the long term it will also get you resentment, hostility, lack of respect, lack of co-operation and so on which, I assume, is what you do not want.
- *The penny has to drop in the other person's mind.* An issue might be very clear in your mind but that is only a starting point. If you want someone else's co-operation it has to be clear in their mind too. Do not take it for granted that the other person sees the issue the same way you see it. Perception tends to be individual, so the chances are they do not.

> *You have only one tool at your disposal – your behaviour.* Unless you are really gifted at telepathy, you have only one tool with which to influence the other person. That tool is your behaviour, so you need to use your behaviour in the same way that skilled people use their tools – selecting the appropriate tool for the job and then using it skilfully.

Let's look at each principle in more detail.

Manipulative influencing has disadvantages for you

There are many ways in which you can influence people. Bullying, cajoling, bribing and seeking sympathy are all effective ways of influencing someone. They work. Make no mistake about it – they can help you get what you want. The problem, however, is that they have *side-effects*. Bullying, cajoling, bribing and seeking sympathy tend to generate resentment, retaliation, defensiveness, disagreement, unhelpfulness, withdrawal of co-operation, lack of 'ownership' of what you have agreed, etc. They get people's backs up. In other words, as well as getting what you want, these behaviours can also get you what you do *not* want. That applies whether the manipulation is intended or unintended.

Intended manipulation

This is the sort of manipulation that can be experienced with pushy salespeople. Its intention is to use spurious logic to paint you into a corner, as it were, so that your only rational way out is to sign their contract. It is characterised by a combination of closed questions, not listening, sometimes interrupting, and by putting words into your mouth that are later 'used in evidence against you'. Here is an example:

Now then, Mr Smith, when did you last review your life assurance?

About 10 years ago – I think.

That's quite some time, Mr Smith. Are you aware of what even modest rates of inflation can do to the value of money over that sort of period?

Well, I can't say I've given it that much thought really. Your colleague said it would be adequate for at least 15 years.

I'm afraid he's no longer with us. But can I assume that you love your family, Mr Smith?

Of course, but –

And that you would be devastated to think of them struggling financially if anything happened to you?

Yes, but we –

And then there are the school fees. Have you separate insurance on the school fees?

No. I thought –

So after inflation and school fees have decimated your insurance there won't be much left. I suggest that if you really love your family you take a look at our new Peace of Mind Plan. I think it's just what you need.

It is possible to use similar tactics with people at work, especially if they are more vulnerable, or junior to you.

Wendy, that report I asked you to do; I've had to bring forward my trip so I'll need it by tomorrow morning. OK?
Tomorrow morning! I'll never get it finished in time.
I'm afraid you'll have to. I need it.
But you said you also wanted the product launch information available by then as well.
Then you'll just have to do both.
But –
Don't you realise that we're all under pressure?
Yes, but –
And did you or did you not tell me that you were a hard worker?
Yes, but –
And at your last appraisal did you or did you not tell me how ambitious you are?
Yes, but –
So the answer is surely, 'Yes, it will be done.' Isn't it?

Intended manipulation is unpleasant. It justifiably attracts a range of adjectives from dishonest to bullying. It leaves the other person feeling cheated, hard done by and resentful. And it destroys your personal credibility!

Unintended manipulation

This also uses spurious logic and closed questions to 'paint you into a corner' but involves less aggression. People who try to influence this way are usually unaware that they are guilty of manipulation. They have probably never been taught to be open and honest when making a request and so have grown up relying on subtle manipulation. Here is a real life example. It concerns a computer operator who was asked to stand in for the shift supervisor and was paid an allowance accordingly. Several months later there was a reorganization and the post of shift supervisor was abolished. There was therefore no post for the computer operator to stand in for. Due to an oversight, however, the salary allowance continued to be paid. Months later someone in the personnel department spotted the anomaly and confirmed with the computer department manager that the allowance should be stopped immediately. All the computer department manager had then to do was to tell the computer operator the bad news. The conversation went like this:

> *. . . so when we abolished the shift supervisor post we should also have stopped the allowance. I'm sorry, but I'm afraid we're going to have to stop paying it with immediate effect.*
> Why should I get a pay cut just because we no longer have shift supervisors?
> *It isn't a pay cut as such. It's just that we'll no longer be paying the allowance.*
> Well, it'll feel like a pay cut to me. I'm relying on that money to pay my mortgage. I've quoted it to the bank manager as part of my gross earnings.
> *Well, I'm afraid I can't really. . .*
> I may not get the mortgage now. What's my fiancée going to say?
> *I'm sure that. . .*
> One minute everything's going all right, then suddenly someone pulls the rug out from under you. How would you like this to happen to you?
> *I wouldn't, but. . .*

You're my manager. I thought you were there to support me.

Well . . . perhaps I could have a word with personnel.

Note the spurious logic employed by the computer operator: calling the loss of the allowance a pay cut, bringing his fiancée into the equation and, the trump card, implying that the manager has let him down. All this logic is designed to make the manager feel responsible for the computer operator's position (unenviable though it is) and guilty for not having a magic wand. Yet on examination the logic is this: 'I didn't check my salary details with you before giving them to the bank manager. That's your fault. My fiancée will be very upset. That's your fault. You wouldn't like this to happen to you, yet you're making it happen to me. That's not fair. Your acting correctly over my pay is the same as a withdrawal of your support for me. Managers should support their staff.'

It is unlikely that the computer operator is trying to manipulate his manager deliberately. He is understandably upset (to the extent that he forgets that, from another angle, he has been receiving money for over a year to which he was not entitled) and so applies 'logic' as he sees it.

Why do we manipulate?

We learn from a very early age that some feelings and emotions are pleasant and that others are uncomfortable and best avoided. Parents, older siblings and other authority figures seem adept at using this fact to influence our behaviour. With carefully chosen words and body language they can make us feel good, bad, happy, sad, and so on. As is often the case, it is the negative feelings that have the greatest impact on us and so give rise to the most memorable learning experiences. We learn that feelings of guilt, embarrassment, etc make us take action to avoid those feelings. We experiment to see if we can make such manipulation as we have experienced work for us too and, gradually, we incorporate the appropriate tactics into our growing repertoire of how to deal with other people. That repertoire we take with us into adulthood.

You probably come across other examples daily. The manager who normally lets a colleague use her secretary whenever he is busy, but who cannot on one occasion, will be greeted with the observation, 'But you always help me out when I'm busy.' The implication is, 'Why have you suddenly changed? People should be consistent.' The manager who delegates a report to a member of staff, and subsequently tells him that he has just promised it will be ready two days early will plead, 'But I've promised: you're not going to make me break a promise, are you?' The implication is 'I've made an unrealistic commitment, but it will be your fault if I have made myself look stupid.' The member of staff who seeks clarification about a hastily delegated task will be told, 'I hope you're not going to make me late for my meeting.' The implication is, 'You're responsible for my poor time management.'

Time and time again we fall for spurious logic, yet at the same time we know that the accompanying feelings of guilt, responsibility, awkwardness, etc should not really be part of the equation. By the time the cerebral dust settles we know that we have been manipulated and feel bad about it.

It is easier to spot when it is happening to us than when we do it to someone else. Have you ever 'encouraged' someone to do something by belittling them? You are unlikely to get what you want. Have you ever sought a colleague's co-operation by making them feel sorry for you? You are unlikely to find a willing helper. Motivation is a door that is locked on the inside. As the saying goes, you can wish someone a merry Christmas but you cannot insist they have one. Manipulation, whether intended or unintended, rarely helps you achieve what you want in both the short and the long term.

How does positive influencing differ?

Whether manipulating or positively influencing, you are trying to get someone else to do what you want. The difference is that manipulation uses tactics designed around spurious logic, negative feelings, or both, while positive influencing relies upon openness and honesty. Even allowing for the fact that some people may not want to be persuaded, positive influencing is likely to prove more productive than will manipulation. Manipulation will give rise to bad feelings about you and what it is you want the other person to do; their commitment to the course of action will diminish as it gradually dawns on them that they have been manipulated. On the other hand, positive influencing, because it uses openness and honesty which show respect to the other person, makes it easy for them to appreciate your point of view. If they accept your invitation to agree with you, their commitment is likely to be sustained into the future. The basic message is this: behaviours that respect the other person produce better results than manipulation.

The penny has to drop in the other person's mind

For someone to be convinced of something, the 'penny has to drop' in their mind. That is, it has to make sense to *them*. No matter how obvious something is to you, if you want someone's help, co-operation or agreement, it has to be obvious to them.

Fairly obvious really. What is not so obvious is that just because it makes sense to you does not automatically mean it will make sense to them. You cannot *force* the penny to drop in their mind. What you can do, however, is to *cause* them to *think,* and that thinking process can cause the penny to drop.

You have only one 'tool' available to you to make them think – your behaviour. What often happens, however, is that when we are faced with someone who does not see what, to us, is blindingly obvious, we jump to the conclusion that they are daft, obstinate or just plain awkward. We see the fault as theirs and attempt to overcome their obstinacy or stupidity with manipulation. We attempt to 'bulldoze' them, 'out-logic' them, make them feel guilty, awkward or fearful of disagreeing. Even if we succeed in gaining their agreement, influencing in this way delivers someone with the grudging acceptance of a conscript rather than the motivation of a volunteer.

Imagine a situation in which a salesman is trying to sell something to a prospective customer. The salesman knows that the product is right for the customer; he can see exactly what benefits it will bring. He also knows the price is fair and that if the customer uses the product correctly it will pay for itself in no time. The fact that the salesman knows all these things is immaterial. It is the customer who has to know them, because it is the customer who will make the decision whether or not to buy.

How easily the customer comes to the same conclusion depends on many factors, such as whether the customer has the same depth of understanding as the salesman, is a willing prospect, or is being 'cold called', and so on. What we can say is that if the salesman assumes that just because *he* can see the logic of his argument the *customer* also will, he may soon be disappointed!

Yet this assumption is a mistake that many of us make all too often. It is easy to forget that when trying to influence someone we are in a similar position to the salesman. We may not be selling something in the literal sense of the word, but we still want someone else to 'buy into' our way of thinking – which is another way of saying that we want them to agree with us genuinely and voluntarily. Hence they, and not just we, have to see the logic of our argument. It sounds fairly obvious when explained in this way, so why do we not follow these principles as often as we could?

Using your behaviour to cause the penny to drop in their mind requires both patience and skill. It is not loved by people who are too busy or too self-important! My reaction to such people is twofold. First, if you cannot find time to do the job properly can you realistically find time to do it twice or three times? Because that may be the price of not influencing the other person successfully first time around. Second, if what you want is not dependent on the other person's co-operation, why are you trying to influence them in the first place? So you might as well influence them effectively. After all, it is in your own interests to use your behaviour in such a way that you get closer to the outcome you want, and farther away from the outcome you do not want.

You have only one tool at your disposal – your behaviour

After you have tried all the alternatives such as telepathy and ouija boards you will come to only one conclusion – if you want to influence someone, you have to use your behaviour. And here comes the big point. *You have to gear your behaviour to the outcome you want to achieve rather than to your dominant thoughts and emotions.* Most people do it the other way round. They gear their behaviour to their dominant thoughts and emotions rather than to the outcome they want to achieve. Emotionally, you may want to call them a stupid idiot, an obstinate swine or a person whose mental state is clearly two sandwiches short of a picnic. That may make you feel better (short term) but will make the task of influencing them more difficult and hence make you feel worse (long term).

Think of it this way. You have just moved into a new home and are starting to personalise it. You notice a large screw in the wall from which the previous occupant hung a picture. You want to take the screw out of the wall. So you open up your tool kit, which contains several different screwdrivers. You take the one you use habitually and try to remove the screw. The screw has been screwed in so tightly, and your habitually used screwdriver is such a poor fit in the screw head, that the screwdriver keeps slipping out, burring the screw head and making it even more difficult to remove. Instead of replacing your habitually used screwdriver and selecting another that would be a better fit, you look at the damage caused to the screw head, and realise how much more difficult the task of removing the screw has now become. Very rarely do we review the situation rationally and select another tool to remove the screw. Instead, we curse the screw and the person who originally screwed it into the wall.

Your personal tool kit

We do something similar with our behaviour. We want to influence someone in some way, use the behaviour we habitually use in such situations and, when it does not work, we blame the other person for not listening, being obstinate or as thick as two short planks. It is far better to *use your behavioural repertoire as a tool kit* from which you select the tool (behaviour) most appropriate to the outcome you want to achieve. That is especially important because every time you use your behaviour it triggers a response in the other person.

Triggers and responses

Some behaviours trigger positive responses and some trigger negative ones. So if you listen actively to understand someone, they are more inclined to listen to you. On the other hand, if you make a counter-attack (responding to someone's attack on you with an attack on them) they are likely to attack again, sending the conversation into a downward 'defend/attack' spiral. Some responses are relatively predictable while others are unpredictable. If you probe, for example, you are likely to receive information. If you disagree with someone, however, the other person could respond in any number of ways. They could disagree with your disagreement, provide more information to support their case, suggest an alternative, ask you what you would do, capitulate, or respond in a host of other ways. It makes sense, therefore, to avoid behaviours that trigger negative or unpredictable responses and to get into the habit of using behaviours that trigger predictable positive responses.

So, there are the three fundamental principles on which positive influencing is based. How do you feel about them? My experience of teaching influencing skills is that although most people have never actually thought about such principles before, once they have heard them they feel as if long-held, but uncoordinated thoughts have just crystallised into a coherent whole.

Why do we get it wrong?
There are several reasons. First, we rarely see a good role model. We have grown up with parents who tried to alter our behaviour by talking at us; schoolteachers who tried to teach us by talking at us; and managers who tried to motivate us by talking at us – rather than by discussing with us and trying to see our point of view. Second,

we make the same assumptions as poor salespeople. We assume that just because we can see the logic of our case the other person will see it too. Third, we are unaware that our behaviour tends to trigger a response in the other person and we are unaware, therefore, that the unproductive response from the other person is actually being triggered by ourselves!

Pause for thought

Before you move on, you may like to ask yourself to what extent these principles show themselves in your current behaviour. On page 15 there are 10 questions. Answer them honestly and see what they reveal about you, then read the points below.

- If you ticked 'rarely' for most answers, well done (although you might want to ask someone else for their opinion to check you are not being too generous to yourself).
- If you ticked 'sometimes' for most answers, you will find the core skills useful in helping you adopt more of a 'pulling' style of influencing.
- If you ticked 'often' for most answers, well done for honesty! It is worth asking yourself, however, to what extent you agree with the content of this section. If you are not converted to this way of thinking, exactly what are your objections? Do they pass the TSR Test? Do other people agree? How would truly effective influencers you know score on the questionnaire? What do they do that is different from what you do?

When trying to influence someone, how often do you: (tick the appropriate box)

		Rarely	Sometimes	Often
1	feel they are being deliberately obstinate or stupid or slow?	☐	☐	☐
2	use prescriptive language, making suggestions sound like instructions?	☐	☐	☐
3	find it odd that they cannot see the benefits in what you are suggesting?	☐	☐	☐
4	find yourself talking more than the other person?	☐	☐	☐
5	find it is quicker to 'browbeat' or 'out-logic' the other person to get what you want?	☐	☐	☐
6	use jargon that is not necessarily shared by the other person?	☐	☐	☐
7	find yourself attaching labels such as 'obstinate' or 'stupid' to the other person?	☐	☐	☐
8	feel as if you just do not understand 'where the other person is coming from'?	☐	☐	☐
9	engage in debate during which you promote your own case and deliberately avoid finding out more about the other person's view?	☐	☐	☐
10	find yourself increasingly at odds with the prevailing views of other people?	☐	☐	☐

2

Core skill one
persuasive probing

Let's get straight to the point. *Probing is brilliant!* It is the 'Swiss Army penknife' in your interpersonal skills toolkit. It will do hundreds of different jobs, get you out of all sorts of scrapes and it looks pretty good too. It is without doubt the most useful and versatile interpersonal skill to possess. Its benefits are numerous:

- It *provides information* that you can use to persuade the other person. It can reveal what is important to them, what their concerns are and even what terminology will make them feel comfortable with you.
- It can *cause the other person to think about what you want them to think about.* So if you think your idea is right for them, instead of telling them, you can cause them to think about it by asking them the right questions. You can even help them visualise it and come to the right conclusion themselves.
- It *keeps you in control of the pace and direction of the conversation.* Most people are pre-programmed to answer questions. Decades of experience with

parents and schoolteachers has taught us that
when we are asked a question we should
answer it. So all the time you are probing, even
though the other person is doing most of the
talking, because they are talking about what
you have just asked them, you are in control of
both the pace and direction of the conversation.
(Unless, of course, you are talking to
professional politicians who usually begin their
answers with the phrase, 'That's an interesting
question but what is even more important is
blah, blah, blah, so let me make this absolutely
clear blah, blah, blah.')

It can *signal, very gently, that you disagree with them.*
The big problem with a straightforward
disagreement is that it triggers a defensive
reaction in the other person. Instead of finding
out why you disagree, or even listening to you
explaining why you disagree, their thoughts go
into overdrive as they try to work out why you
are disagreeing, what your disagreement means
to them, or what else they can say to persuade
you. In short, your disagreement stops them
listening. A carefully placed question, however,
will not only signal that you are not actually
agreeing with them but will cause them to think
through their proposal and perhaps spot the
very reason why you cannot agree.

It *can provide much needed thinking time* when you
are being put under pressure. The fastest speech
on record was given by Canadian Sean Shannon
in 1995, when he recited Hamlet's soliloquy in

23.8 seconds. That is about 650 words per minute. That is very fast. President Kennedy once gave a speech at over 300 words a minute. That is fast. Most of us speak at only 160 to 200 words per minute. That is quite slow. Yet even Sean Shannon is slow compared to how fast we can think. We can think at the equivalent of *several thousand* words a minute. You may have noticed that having to think about what you are saying while you are saying it is not easy. In fact when you are under pressure, it can add to the panic! That is why trying to talk your way out of a pressure situation usually only adds to the pressure. You have *no* thinking time; the other person has *lots* of it. By asking questions, however, (and remember, most of us are pre-programmed to respond to them) you get the other person talking (at 160 to 200 words per minute) while you think (at several thousand words per minute). Bingo! You now have enough time to marshal your thoughts.

- It can *give you the appearance of being knowledgeable* about a subject. Perversely, in other people's minds, asking someone questions about a topic makes you appear more knowledgeable about that topic than others who just talk about it. In fact you may not be, but you will have given that impression without resorting to the high risk strategy of bulls**t (which positive influencers always avoid).

- It can *turn you into a proficient conversationalist.* To paraphrase Voltaire, not only is the secret of being boring to say everything, but often in casual conversations you may not know what to say. So, unless you do something incredibly interesting, like extinguish fires on oil rigs or make the gadgets used by James Bond, you are better off listening to the other person. Surprisingly, once you start probing, other people can be very interesting. And, once again, something rather perverse happens. Just because you have shown interest in the other person, they regard *you* as interesting. So, whether your goal is to build rapport with the other person, to avoid being the only one at a conference with no one to talk to, or just to survive a boring dinner party when you are seated next to the only molecular physicist you have ever met, probing comes to your rescue.

Above all, probing can *make the other person feel comfortable with both the process and the outcome of the conversation* with you. Generally, most human beings prefer talking to listening to such an extent that, given the choice, that is what we will do. We also like the feeling of being listened to. It is a positive, gratifying experience. And, if the person listening to us is just about to recommend a solution to a problem, we feel they understand us sufficiently well to make a sound recommendation. Probing really is the bee's knees.

These are the real and tangible benefits of probing – if you do it effectively. Unfortunately, most of us have an in-built handicap when it comes to probing – time travel!

The time-travel handicap

I do not, of course, mean literal time travel. It is just that with the other person talking at fewer than 200 words a minute and you thinking at several thousand words a minute, we have a lot of spare thinking capacity. This makes it easy for us to 'think ahead' in the conversation and (and this bit is really important) to make statements or to ask questions that *confirm our thinking* rather than to *explore and understand the other person's thinking*, which negates all the benefits of persuasive probing listed above. There are four solutions to the time-travel handicap.

Solution 1 – Ask the right questions

The most useful types of questions are open questions. An open question is one to which it is difficult to reply 'yes' or 'no'; such as, 'How do you feel about that suggestion?' or 'Why is that a problem for you?', or 'What would you do if you had to make this decision yourself?' Open questions have the potential to uncover a lot of information.

To gauge the kind of questions you ask, think of the ratio of talking between you and the other person. In a disciplinary interview you might need to do 70 per cent of the talking; in an appraisal discussion only 40 per cent; when selling only 30 per cent and when counselling only 10 per cent. Questions such as, 'How do you feel about . . .?' or 'In what way...?' tend to get the other person talking, providing valuable and genuine information. They show that you are interested in the other person and their situation. They also encourage a ratio of talking in favour of the other person, so they feel, correctly, they are making a big contribution to the conversation. There is no guarantee of this, however. Shy people can still find a way to give a closed answer to an open question, so a little later in this section I will show you how to combine different types of question to encourage even the shyest person to talk.

The opposite of an open question is a closed one. Because closed questions tend to narrow down a conversation rather than open it up, some people on courses learn that open questions are good and closed questions are bad. That is like saying that hammers are good and screwdrivers are bad; not so. They are simply tools designed for different jobs. Where open questions are good for *exploring*, closed questions are good for *checking*. I include closed questions in the 'careful handling' category, however, because it is all too easy to use them incorrectly.

The problem is that our brains work incredibly fast – much faster than the speed of speech coming from the person to whom we are listening. It is easy therefore for our minds to run ahead and to ask questions that check what we are thinking rather than find out what the other person is thinking. Let us take an example with a member of staff who has just returned from a meeting. During the debriefing after the meeting, when the member of staff tells the boss how she responded to the finance manager's questions, the boss might ask one of two questions: 'Did you say that because you weren't sure of the answer?' or

'Why did you say that?' The first question is closed and invites the member of staff to confirm what is in the boss's mind. The second question is open and invites the member of staff to explain what is in her mind.

With the open question there is a very good chance that the boss will get the genuine information she seeks. With the closed question that chance is much smaller. Furthermore, a succession of open questions sends a message saying, 'I'm genuinely interested in what's in *your* mind; I'm listening.' A succession of closed questions, on the other hand, sends a message saying, 'I'm more concerned with what's in *my* mind; I'm not listening.' Closed questions are best reserved for checking information, which lets us know how to proceed. If the debrief on the meeting goes like this:

> *Did the finance manager behave as predicted?*
> Exactly.

you will want to handle the conversation one way. If it goes like this:

> *Did the finance manager behave as predicted?*
> Not at all.

you will want to handle it differently. These examples occur at the beginning of a conversation. You may also want to check at the end of a conversation.

Questioning shy people

Closed questions are often easier to answer than open ones, and so can be used to encourage a shy person to 'open up'. Here is an example. Imagine a manager conducting a routine appraisal with a shy member of staff. As you read it, look at how the initial open questions produce minimal response and how the manager then employs closed questions to get the conversation moving by teasing information from the member of staff.

How do you feel you've performed in the last six months?
All right.
How would you describe your performance?
OK.
Would you say you've improved?
I hope so.
In every aspect of your work?
I don't know.
What about the way you deal with customers. Is that better or worse?
Better...I think.
I agree. You seem more confident with customers than you used to be. Why is that?
I know the products better now. And telephone techniques. That course you sent me on taught me a lot. And Jean: she's been coaching me. And I've been taking the manuals home in the evenings to make sure I understand them.

In this example, the initial open question, contrary to what many people are taught, produces a closed answer, so the manager paraphrases the question and repeats it. This tactic usually produces something – but not in this example. So he then asks a closed question which, being easier for a shy person to answer, produces a small response. The manager then asks a forced-choice question but, as with the closed question, it is reasonably easy to answer and so receives a useful response. Having warmed up the member of staff, the manager then tries another open question that finally produces valuable information.

Questions best avoided

There are two main types of question that rarely, if ever, produce positive results and are best avoided because they leave the other person with the feeling that they are being manipulated.

- A *leading question* is one that tells the other person how you expect or how you prefer them to answer. So 'How do you feel when that happens?', which is a genuine open question, becomes 'You don't like it when that happens, do you?'; 'What are your views on this proposal?' becomes 'Am I right in assuming that everyone agrees with this proposal?' Although there are occasions when leading questions can be used successfully to open a conversation (such as when a child falls over heavily and the parent asks, 'That hurt you, didn't it?') it is really more of a statement than a genuine inquiry. Also, whatever it is that we are referring to has to be obvious (such as the graze on the child's knee). Otherwise, leading questions are at best presumptive and at worst downright rude. So even if you want to use one genuinely, you are on safer ground if you ask an open question.
- *Evaluative questions* are heavily laden with

comment. 'How long are you going to cling to those outdated views?' is just another way of saying, 'I think you're way out of date.' 'Isn't that rather a naive way of looking at it?' is just another way of saying, 'I think you're being naive.' All we do with evaluative questions is antagonise the other person; they are likely to counter-attack or withdraw from an active part in the conversation, depending on how aggressive or submissive they are.

At this stage you may be saying to yourself, 'But that's exactly the way television and radio interviewers question people, and they don't have any trouble getting the other person to talk.' So let me make a few points. First, TV and radio interviewers often present the sort of questions that are in the minds of the public. Second, they sometimes want to be provocative. Third, they are usually interviewing someone who is more than willing to talk. In fact the interviewer's problem is often to try and get the interviewee to stop talking, or at least to talk in answer to the question. My advice, therefore, is not to take TV and radio interviewers as an example of how to do it!

Solution 2 – In-depth probing

Another aspect of the time-travel problem is that, when we think we are listening we are really just waiting for our turn to talk. We are looking for a gap to make our next point, formulating our next question or sticking rigidly to our pre-set mental agenda, irrespective of the information coming from the other person. So, in addition to using more open questions than closed ones, we need to think of probing *in depth*. Instead of asking a question, getting an answer and moving on, we need to ask a question and probe into the answer we receive, and then to probe into that answer and then to probe into that answer too; preferably, to about three levels.

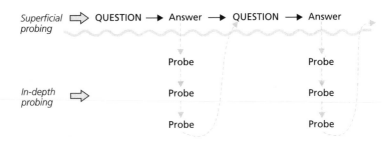

We can do that with straightforward open questions or we can use *reflective questions*. When reflecting, you send the other person's words back to them, either verbatim or paraphrased, with a slight inflection in your tone of voice at the end, signifying that your reflection is really a question. If you have never come across reflecting, this may sound odd. So here is a short example to illustrate reflecting. The example concerns a colleague with a problem who approaches another colleague for help.

Have you got a minute, Jean?
Yes. What can I do for you?
Well, I'm not sure how to begin.
It's a bit tricky?
Yes. I've been offered promotion to head Customer Services and I'm not sure about it.
It's got you confused?

I'll say. I want the job but...well...I'm just not sure.

The job has advantages and disadvantages?

Yes, it's a good career move and the extra money will be great but it's the hours I'd have to work.

The hours are a problem?

Yes. I've got a young family, you see, and I'm not sure about collecting them from school. I don't know what arrangements the school makes for working parents who can't get there at normal going-home time.

If the school has facilities to look after the kids there is no problem, but if it doesn't you'd have to find an alternative?

That's right . . . I suppose the first thing to do is to speak to the school and then, if they can't help, to check out alternatives. Jean, you've been very helpful. You've helped me think this through. Thanks.

In fact Jean made no contribution to the conversation other than to reflect back what her colleague had said. The effect on her colleague, however, was to feel reassured that she was being listened to, to think through her problem, to put it into some sort of perspective, and to generate alternatives herself.

Although reflecting is most commonly used in counselling situations it has other applications too. When staff are being coached, for example, reflecting encourages them to think through issues for themselves, to consider the consequences of proposed action, and to develop their own solutions. When conducting a selection interview, reflecting encourages the interviewee to provide more and 'deeper' information. For example:

And when my boss was in hospital I ran the department.
You had sole responsibility?
Not at first. The divisional manager insisted I clear everything with him but when he saw that I could handle it, he let me get on with it.
He gave you complete freedom?
Yes, for all routine matters like work scheduling, budget control and staff recruitment, but if I wanted to fire anyone or make any capital expenditure I had to let him know.
You just informed him?
No, I had to make a proper case to him, but in the six months my boss was in hospital the divisional manager accepted all my recommendations. That's why I want this job, you see. I think I've proved myself, but now that my boss is back from hospital my authority is back to what it was before.

Even in general conversation, the effect is the same – more information that goes a little bit deeper. So you need never run out of something to say. All you have to do is probe.

Solution 3 – Listen actively

We like listeners. We feel good about *them* because they make *us* feel good. Whenever I have asked people to list the qualities of their best-ever boss, colleague, subordinate, friend, or neighbour, listening has always featured high on the list. People also talk more to good listeners (according to one piece of research, about twice as much). But you have to listen *actively* rather than *passively*. Understanding the difference between active listening and passive listening is easier if you understand the overall communication process.

Not a lot of people know that!

Although we have been communicating for as long as we can remember, few of us stop to think what the communication process involves. If you are telepathic it is quite simple.

If you are not, it is much more complex.

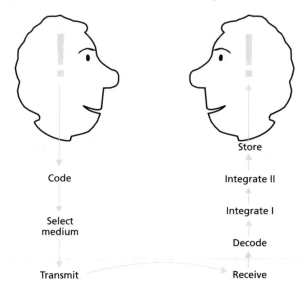

So first, the other person has to *convert their concept or idea into codes* (words, sounds, gestures, facial expressions, etc).

Second, they have to *select a transmission medium* that they feel is appropriate. It might be a letter, a memo, an e-mail, a formal report, a casual meeting, a formal meeting, a telephone call, etc. Third, they have to *choose an appropriate time to transmit* the message. Fourth, with a bit of luck, you are as receptive as they hoped and you can *receive their transmission*. This is where the active listening comes in because, fifth, you have to *decode their message*. Even if the message is not confused with irrelevant diversions, 'ums' and 'ers', beating about the bush, in-your-face bluntness, jargon, similes, etc, decoding the message may not be that straightforward. Sixth, you have to perform two *integration processes*. The first is to string the various bits of their message into a *coherent whole* and the second is to *relate* their message to information already stored in your brain so that you can appreciate it, analyse it, criticise it, agree or disagree with it etc. Finally, you have to *store their message* in such a way that you can *retrieve it later*.

Consider listening in the light of this process. If you listen passively – that is, *without engaging the speaker in dialogue*, you cannot query parts of the message, check your understanding, seek clarification, and so on. Receiving the bits of information will not be a problem (as long as there is no interference such as noise or visual distractions). Decoding could be a problem if the speaker uses codes with which you are unfamiliar. For example a computer with a '686 chip' or with a speed of '66 MHz' no doubt means a lot to people who understand it; a 'permanently inoperative hostile combatant' no doubt means a lot to someone in the military; 'touching base' and 'running it up the flagpole to see if anyone salutes it' is no doubt very precise terminology to people who are familiar with those phrases. Integrating can be a problem if the speaker's thoughts are unstructured or if the speaker has a different frame of reference from you. Storing and recalling can be problems if the messages are unclear to you.

When listening actively you *engage the speaker in dialogue and use behaviours that help you listen in the full sense of the word*. Look at the table below and ask yourself which behaviours people might associate with you. If it is 'not listening' behaviours, it is worth changing them. If it is 'passive listening' behaviours, you have only to add the 'active listening' behaviours to overcome the time-travel problem.

Not listening	Passive listening	Active listening
Interrupting	Helpful eye contact	Helpful eye contact
Being distracted	and looking	and looking
Doodling	receptive	receptive
Lengthy note-taking	Making encour-	Reflecting
Closing your eyes	aging sounds and	Probing
Yawning	gestures	Making appropriate
Clock-watching and		comments
making 'hurry up'		Summarising
gestures		Checking under-
Changing the subject		standing
abruptly		

Listening in this way has several benefits:

- The other person finds you satisfying to talk to because we like people who listen, who appear interested in us, who make an effort to understand us rather than jumping to conclusions, and so on.
- You clear up any 'decoding' problems and find it easier to integrate and store the other person's message.
- You find the listening process more satisfying because you are involved in it.
- You are building or maintaining a relationship with the speaker in a way that passive listening cannot achieve.

Solution 4 – The persuasive funnel

Using open questions, probing, and listening actively are useful tools in everyone's interpersonal tool kit. You can gain even more influencing potential from them, however, if you structure them into a coherent whole. That structure is the 'persuasive funnel'.

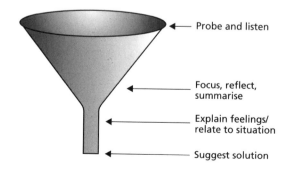

- Probe and listen
- Focus, reflect, summarise
- Explain feelings/ relate to situation
- Suggest solution

Whether you are trying to sell a product or an idea to someone, or resolve some conflict, the four steps in this structure will help.

- In step 1 you *probe and listen*. This will be relatively easy, as customers and people with whom you have a problem are usually keen to tell you about what they want. As you listen, you probe. At this stage, you are not only making the other person feel good, you are gathering a lot of useful information that you can use when it is your turn to talk. In conflict situations particularly, it is a lot easier to get the other person to listen to and understand you if you have first listened to and understood them. It can require a lot of patience to sit there listening to the other person, so just relax knowing that the other person is telling you what you need to know in order to suggest something that they are more likely to accept.

- When you feel they have told you as much as they are going to, *summarise* (step 2) to check that you have understood them fully. Check that they feel your summary is accurate, (especially if you have used the opportunity of the summary to focus their attention on any aspect of what they have said that just might show your suggestion in a more attractive light).

- Step 3 will vary, depending on whether you are selling something or resolving conflict. If you are selling, *relate it to the situation or criteria* that the other person has already described to you in steps 1 and 2. If you are resolving conflict, *explain your feelings*. This may sound strange but no one can disagree with your feelings in the same way they can disagree with a fact or with a point of view. This makes the other person more receptive to step 4.

In step 4 you *suggest your desired outcome*. You can continue to probe in this step to help the other person visualise what your suggestion will mean to them. For example ask, 'What would you do with that extra time?', or 'What could you achieve with an extra member of staff?'

Small differences of opinion can drive a wedge between people intent on promoting their suggestion to the exclusion of all else. Listening to the other person's case before you advocate yours, however, is in your own interests because it is easier to make yourself understood if you have first understood the other person. Seeking to understand other people can make you more tolerant without causing you to compromise on critical issues. It can make you selective about the issues you feel require attention. It can also encourage you to listen actively and genuinely – behaviour that never fails to enhance someone's personal credibility. The basic message, therefore, of *seek first to understand and you will know better how to make yourself understood* is embodied within the persuasive funnel.

Here are two examples. The first example shows how an attempt to influence can go wrong if the persuasive funnel is not used, and the second shows how it can go right if the funnel is used. The situation concerns a training manager trying to persuade a research manager to invest time, money and effort in establishing Personal Development Plans (PDPs) for all his professional staff. The company is commercial, and Research is one of the sales divisions. Here is example one. (The training manager speaks first.)

Thank you for seeing me, John. As you know, I'm keen to get PDPs into all divisions by the end of the year.
That's as may be, but I'm taking on no new initiatives at the moment.
I'd think carefully. Personal development is a major issue in the company at the moment, you know.
I know that, and I'm not saying I won't do it. I'm just saying that, at the moment, I've got enough on my plate trying to stay competitive. There are quite a few university sales teams out there trying to pinch my customers – and in some cases being successful.
But, surely, keeping skills up to date is important to you?
Of course it is, but, as I said, keeping customers is even more important.
But how will your staff feel if they see other divisions implementing PDPs while you're not?
And how will they feel if they are made redundant because of falling revenue? I think they'd rather have a job than a PDP, don't you?
That's not a long-term view, though, is it, John?
I can drain the swamp when I've shot the crocodiles. In the meantime, I can't do anything about PDPs. Maybe next year.

Example two follows. (Again, the training manager speaks first.)

Thank you for seeing me, John. As you know, I want to discuss PDPs with you but you mentioned over the phone that you had other priorities at the moment. So, to ensure that I understand, can we talk about the research division in general?

OK. What do you want to know?

Why don't we start with those other priorities? What takes up most of your time at the moment?

That's an easy one: trying to fend off the competition.

How is the competition changing?

It's getting tougher. Universities are having so much funding cut that they are becoming quite aggressive in sales to make up revenue. As they still receive some state funding, however, they can generally undercut us.

How are you and your team responding to that?

We stress our experience compared with that of universities. Our people tend to have more industrial experience.

How does that make a difference?

Our people are more likely to spot problems early on in a project. They can also identify short cuts. That can save time and money.

In what way will things change in the future?

I think we'll lose more of the bread-and-butter contracts. We can't really compete on cost. That means going for the high-value projects.

And what is the best way of competing for those?

We have to ensure that we get the right experience, stay at the cutting edge of technology and that we present our knowledge, skills and experience in such a way that we stand head and shoulders above the competition.

So you need to present the knowledge, skills and experience of your staff as a competitive advantage?

Exactly.

And what are you doing to ensure that their knowledge, skills and experience develop the way you want so as to give you that competitive advantage in the future?

Well...just relying on people learning from their jobs I suppose...and doing the right postgraduate qualifications...going on the right courses. That sort of thing.

Are people getting the right experience?

I'm not sure anyone can say that they're getting exactly the right experience.

How do you present it to customers?

In a kind of CV for each staff member who would be working on a contract.

How do customers react to the CVs?

We do need to present them better. I'm aware of that.

And what's the staff situation like?

At the moment it's OK but we've just done appraisals and I know that if we don't help people manage their careers better then there will be problems in the future.

It sounds as if you need a way of managing people's careers, experience, qualifications and training so that they are fully

satisfied, and customers are impressed enough to give you
the high-value contracts.
You've got a magic wand, have you?
No, just a suggestion. What you're describing is exactly
what PDPs are designed to achieve.
You'll have to explain that to me.
I'd be glad to. Let's start with your business needs...

The first example shows no desire to see what the research manager might need; it promotes only what the training manager wants to sell. Consequently the research manager finds it easy to resist. In the second example, the research manager has nothing to resist because all the training manager is doing is asking him questions about his priorities; because those questions are open rather than closed there is no hint of manipulation. The training manager is, however, 'rounding up' vital information. He is spotting a 'reason' for the research manager to 'buy into' his way of thinking, and also the benefits, or the 'results', that the research manager will 'buy'. Furthermore, at no time does he come across as 'pushy': the ratio of talking is well within the research manager's favour and there is no dominance of closed questions either.

If we want to adopt a *positive* influencing approach, we have to remember that:

- It is the other person who has to make the decision, not us (after all, we want them to buy into our way of thinking, not vice versa). The penny has to drop in their mind.
- People 'buy' things to fulfil needs.

- What we are offering has features and benefits; the features are characteristics of the offer, while the benefits are what those characteristics will do for the other person.
- If we probe and listen we may be able to gather enough information to spot reasons why the other person should agree with us, and we can then present our offer in terms of the benefits they will receive. In doing so, the process is likely to be more satisfying to the other person than if we tried to persuade them in the traditional sense.

Using these lessons

- You might be saying that it is not easy sitting there asking questions when you know that the only logical course of action is for the other person to agree to do what you want. The answer can be as plain as a pikestaff to anyone with even a modicum of common sense. If you find yourself thinking such thoughts, remind yourself of something. Think of the last time you went to buy something, really took a dislike to the salesperson, and walked out – even though the product or service on offer was the best for you. You acted emotionally; you acted irrationally; but so what? It is your money! The sales process has to proceed in a way that customers are happy with. Influencing situations have to proceed in such a way that the person who is being asked to accept something is happy with it.

- Probing may fail to uncover anything of value! The training manager may find that the research department is not yet ready culturally to make a decent job of Personal Development Plans. The training manager may still try to 'close the sale' but his chances of success are minimal. Even if he does succeed, the research manager's satisfaction levels will quickly diminish and the relationship will not be sustained.

- Like all tools, the persuasive funnel needs to be used in appropriate situations. You may be asking, 'But what about those situations where you have to persuade someone to do something in which there is absolutely no benefit to them, such as delegating a menial task? How can you use this persuasive funnel with them? The answer is, you don't! It would be the wrong tool. If there is absolutely no benefit to the other person and you behave as if there is, you will come across as patronising and manipulative. If the other person really has no choice in the matter why pretend that they have? You will be better advised to treat the other person openly, honestly and respectfully (which is positive) and use two of the other core skills – being assertive and building rapport – because most people can spot a phony a mile off. Save the persuasive funnel for situations where you need to persuade someone to accept your way of thinking, where they can turn you down if they

want to, and where their commitment is
essential to long-term success.

This approach does work. Here is a personal story. Many
years ago I decided to buy a burglar alarm for my home
and had several burglar alarm salespeople come to visit
me over a period of days. Two of them told me how
fantastic their burglar alarms were, how sensitive the
detectors were, and how many decibels the alarm registered. The third salesperson told me very little to begin
with. Instead he said, 'I'd like to divide our conversation
into three parts. I'd like to have a look at your house to
make sure I can specify the right configuration for your
needs. I'd also like to tell you about our alarms because
we believe they are very good ones. But first, I'd like to
ask you why you want a burglar alarm?' After I had
answered that question he had another, and another, and
another. The questions, I am sure, were intended to provide him with the information he needed to sell to me. By
the time we had finished, however, I was convinced of
something: I did not want to buy a burglar alarm. What I
wanted to buy was peace of mind! The meeting ended
with my insisting on movement detectors in rooms in
which he thought it was unnecessary to have them, even
though it increased the cost (and his commission) compared with what he believed was necessary.

The first two salespeople had tried to sell to me in the traditional sense of the word. I was on the receiving end of
their 'sales pitch'. I was uninvolved and kept my defences
high. The third had not tried to sell me anything in the traditional sense of the word, but the process of his asking

me questions caused me to crystallise my thoughts and identify the outcome I wanted – despite his protests. I was also happy to recommend him to friends and neighbours because he was not a 'pushy' salesman.

3

Core skill two
being assertive

What is assertiveness?

Assertiveness is a subject with many facets. Although it has been seen traditionally as a way of enhancing the self-esteem and skills of people who were having difficulty handling life's problems, it has emerged as a topic of relevance to management, leadership, teamwork, selling, negotiating and, of course, influencing. Assertiveness can help us in many ways related to positive influencing:

- being more persistent
- improving our tolerance of others when trying to get to the heart of a problem
- protecting ourselves from attempted manipulation.

The fight-or-flight response

Assertiveness can be approached from a variety of directions, but one of the most illustrative is to begin with the fight-or-flight response. This is the reaction that takes place within our bodies to prepare us for action when we are threatened. It is something bred in us over the millennia. Imagine a caveman or -woman strolling around a corner and coming face to face with a sabre-toothed tiger. If the caveman or -woman reacted casually to the danger, they would be eaten. If, on the other hand, they were especially quick at clubbing the tiger or running away, they would live to reproduce. The 'mechanism' that gets people ready to fight or to run is the fight-or-flight response.

When we are threatened, adrenalin is pumped into the bloodstream, enabling us to react physically. All very useful stuff when you are faced with a sabre-toothed tiger. As I said, this fight-or-flight response has been bred into all of us. It is a great way of coping with threat. It even comes into play, however, when faced with interpersonal conflict, triggering aggressive or submissive behaviour.

We have another coping mechanism as well – our *verbal reasoning ability*. We can use our brains and our language to talk through conflict. Unfortunately, there is a problem. In our formative years our verbal ability is still developing, so we receive more practice in our fight-or-flight response than we do in our verbal reasoning ability. So, as we grow we get more practice at aggressive and submissive behaviours than we do at assertive ones. But what do these three behaviours look like? Look at the table on pages 45–46.

Behaviour	Characteristics
Aggressive	Keen to win, even at others' expense
	Overly concerned with own needs
	Excessive eye contact used to intimidate
	Loud, obtrusive or threatening voice
	Expansive posture
	Invades others' space
	Finger-wagging and finger-pointing at others
	Blunt
	Quick to blame others
	Interrupts frequently
	Authoritarian
	Persists to the point of stubbornness
	Uses sarcasm, criticism, ridicule and patronising language to win a point
	Makes requests sound like orders
	Quickly escalates a situation
Passive or submissive	Keen to avoid confrontation even at own expense
	Overly concerned with 'permission' to act
	Minimal eye contact, usually down and away
	Quiet, hesitant voice
	Defensive, shrinking posture
	Nervous hand-rubbing and fidgeting
	Beats about the bush, drops hints, avoids getting to the point
	Quick to blame self
	Makes elaborate excuses and justifications before acting
	Gives in easily
	Seeks sympathy or makes people feel guilty to get his or her way

Assertive	Keen to stand up for own rights while accepting that others have rights too
	Concerned with principles and the needs of the situation to reach agreement
	Enough eye contact, especially with key words, to demonstrate confidence
	Tone of voice and body language usually moderate, and support message
	Listens, seeks to understand
	Treats people with respect
	Solution-oriented, prepared to compromise
	Straight and to the point without being abrupt
	Prepared to stand up for self and to persist with a point

To behave assertively you have to be able to do two things: *think* assertively and use assertiveness *techniques*.

Who's in charge of your thinking?

Our behaviour is preceded by something – thoughts and feelings. This point is important because it means that our behaviour is more likely to be the result of an unconscious self-fulfilling prophecy than it is to be the result of a deliberate choice. In effect, we allow other people and situations to determine our thoughts. (Ask yourself if being upset or angry when you are stuck in a traffic jam makes the traffic disperse any quicker, or helps you pass the time more productively.)

When we are not in control of our thoughts, and our thoughts determine our behaviour, we are *behaving by default*. Assertive people, on the other hand, manage to take responsibility for their thoughts and *think* assertively. They *select* their behaviour for the outcome they want. This is *behaving by design*. The first step towards taking charge of your thoughts is to reassess how you feel about yourself.

Your relationship with yourself

We all have a set of assumptions about ourselves, about the way it is all right for us to behave in certain situations, about what we are entitled to and what we are not entitled to, and so on. These assumptions affect the way we think, which in turn affects the way we behave. When you assume it is all right to manipulate people to get your way, you will probably come across as aggressive. When you feel you do not have the right to have your views considered, you will probably come across as submissive. When we take responsibility for our thoughts we take responsibility for our actions and start behaving more by design than by default. That makes it easier for us to behave assertively. At this stage, all we need to help us stay assertive, rather than drift into submissiveness or aggressiveness, are a few assertiveness techniques.

Assertiveness techniques

Before looking at the main assertiveness techniques, it is worth emphasising the importance of body language. The wrong tone of voice, for example, will turn your assertive words into aggressive ones; an avoidance of eye contact will turn your assertive statement into a submissive one. So in what follows please remember that the techniques need to be supported by the right body language. Here are the main techniques.

Basic assertion

This means saying what you want or how you feel – *clearly*. This is where most people go wrong; they use emotive language or ramble on. They seem to think that being honest means being so about everything they are thinking at the time. It does not. It means *being honest about what is relevant*. The other person might remind you of your uncle Albert on a bad day, Attila the Hun or an agitated kipper. It does not matter. If that information will hinder rather than help the situation, keep it yourself. 'That's just what my father used to do' is probably irrelevant but 'I wish you'd told me earlier. Telling me at this late stage will cause problems' probably is relevant. Sticking to what is relevant also helps with the other major aid to clarity – *being concise*.

This is particularly important in situations where emotions are running high, because those emotions, by triggering the fight-or-flight response, are sending us down the submissive or aggressive route. On the submissive route we fear conflict and so water down our comments, which lose their impact. On the aggressive route we go in too hard, exaggerate and use the sort of language that makes the other person remember less of what we said and more of how we said it. The emotional element can trigger the other person's fight-or-flight response, sending them down the submissive or aggressive route. The other person may be 'unreasonable' or 'over-emotional' but we still need to achieve an outcome with them.

We need to avoid losing the issue under discussion in a fog of emotion. We need to select terminology that is accurate, easy for us to say, and less likely to be received emotionally by the other person. Consider the following pairs of expressions and ask yourself which is the more accurate, the easier to say, and the more 'palatable' to hear:

'You're just not performing. You've got to pull your socks up.'	'I have some concerns about your performance. I'd like to discuss them with you.'
'You're too lazy.'	'Are you aware that you give the impression of being lazy?'
'What you ought to do is…'	'What would be the effect if you…?'
'According to your staff, you're too detached.	'Are you aware that your staff perceive you as detached?'

Pruning the words to the minimum *consistent with accuracy* never fails to assist clarity. Amazingly, it also makes the words easier to say and to hear.

The three-part sentence

This is a valuable extension of basic assertion. As the name suggests, it is a sentence in three parts.

- In the first part, you show empathy or understanding for the other person.
- In the second, you describe how you feel. Alternatively, in a lengthy discussion, you can refer back to the goal or the needs of the

situation. This second part is quite neat because no one can disagree with your feelings or with what they have already agreed with. This makes them more responsive to the third part ...

■ ... in which you state what you want.

So you may say something like,

'John, I can see this decision has to be made quickly. However, I'm very concerned that it's a significant risk. So I'd like to discuss it in more detail, please.' Or, 'Sally, I know from what you've said that most of this extra workload will fall on your department. However, as we've all agreed, this contract is vital for the company, so I'd like us to agree the action plan now.'

Broken record

The old saying, 'If at first you don't succeed, try, try again,' neatly describes the broken record. It consists of repeating what you want over and over again in response to someone else's attempts to manipulate you. Here is an example. Let us say a salesman is trying to make an appointment with you which you do not want. The conversation, using the broken record, might go like this:

Hi! I'm Mr Pushy from WizBang Computers. I'd like to come and see you. May I make an appointment, please?
I understand you want to see me but I don't want to make an appointment, thank you.
Our computers use state-of-the-art technology and are really competitively priced. You'll love them.

I'm sure I will, but I don't want to make an appointment, thank you.

It's no trouble, honestly. I'm in your area on Tuesday.
Would you prefer morning or afternoon?

I'm sure it is no trouble but I don't want to make an appointment.

I can offer very substantial discounts at the moment.

I'm sure you can but I don't want to make an appointment.

Why not?

I just don't want to make an appointment.

Oh … All right, then. May I send you some literature?

Yes. That would be fine, but I don't want to make an appointment.

Notice that you never once tried to out-argue the salesman; nor were you rude. All you did was to acknowledge what he said and then repeat what it was you wanted, clearly and concisely, without reason or apology. Initially some people feel a little uncomfortable saying the same thing over and over, so I usually point out that you can use the broken record in different ways. You can use it to stand your ground. You can also use it to encourage the other person to come to a compromise and, once you see them moving, you can move too.

Pointing out a consequence

This is where you tell the other person what will happen if something else does not. It is almost a threat but it is not delivered in a threatening manner – just a straightforward statement of cause and effect. It can also be 'sweetened' with a proposal of what you would like to happen:

If you won't agree to help me, I'll have to report you to your boss. I'd prefer it if we could work something out between us.

These are the main assertiveness techniques. If necessary you can combine them in a sequence that gets tougher and tougher but which stays consistently assertive. Here is an example of a conversation between two managers working together on a project team. One manager feels they need to discuss plans soon, while the other sees no urgency:

> *So, because the main summer vacation period falls within the project period, I feel we need to meet this week to agree a schedule. Can we meet this week, please?*
>
> I'm a bit busy right now. I'd like to put it off for a few weeks.
>
> *I feel that will cause problems. I'd like to meet this week, please.*
>
> We've got months for this project. What's the rush?
>
> *I'm concerned about people taking vacations, so I'd like to agree a schedule. Can we meet this week please?*
>
> I really don't have time.
>
> *Time is a problem for everyone but I feel this project is complex enough to warrant priority. You seem not to. Why is that? Because I'd still like to meet this week.*
>
> I just don't see it as that urgent.
>
> *I'm afraid I do, so I'd still like to meet this week.*
>
> I couldn't see you until the week after next at the earliest.
>
> *That's unfortunate because I feel that this project is important. If you can't meet me I'll have to tell the boss that*

he can't have the schedule yet, and why. I'd prefer not to have to do that, so can we meet this week?
Oh...all right.

Assertiveness can help us influence in a variety of ways. Here are the main ones:

- It makes us more persuasive.
- It helps focus on behaviour rather than personality.
- It increases our tolerance of others.
- It protects us from other people's attempts to manipulate us.

Defending yourself against manipulation

We know that when some people try to influence us they do so manipulatively. You can protect yourself against attempted manipulation if you can recognise the main manipulation tactics.

Put-downs

Sarcastic comments, patronisation, belittling remarks and dismissive words are all forms of 'put-down'. They are designed to help the other person 'win' at your expense. When we are on the receiving end of a put-down we usually defend ourselves (submissive) or counter-attack (aggressive). Either way, we achieve little. There are two forms of defence against put-downs. The first is to neutrally *acknowledge* what the other person has said and leave it at that.

They have to be the worst clothes I've ever seen.
They aren't to everyone's taste.

This may sound really strange but it is very, very effective. It is verbal judo, in which a small person can 'throw' a larger one by using their own weight and momentum against them. Your 'attacker' is stopped in their tracks.

The second defence is to *probe*. This puts you more on the attack. 'That colour makes you look sickly' could cause you never to wear it again (flight) or to tell the other person that they have the dress sense of a colour-blind gorilla (fight). It is far more effective however to ask, 'In what way?' If their comment is genuine, albeit badly expressed, they will elaborate, giving you valuable information. If it is designed to make you feel inadequate, they will back off.

> *That has to be the worst tie I've ever seen.*
> What is it about the tie that you dislike?
> *It's so loud.*
> In what way?
> *The colours. I mean, they're so bright.*
> You don't like bright colours?
> *I've nothing against bright colours it's just that…*
> What?
> *Er…I've got to go.*

They usually back off sooner rather than later because your questions have made them think harder than they normally do, while you have not had to be even slightly mentally agile.

Bulldozing

These manipulators do not listen. They move at a fast pace, make assumptions on your behalf and do your thinking for you. They use leading and judgemental questions to 'win'. To counter this manipulation technique, you need a combination of responses. First, you have to change your body language. So, if you are seated, for example, lean forward and clasp your hands on the table in front of you like a news reader. If necessary, hold up a hand as if stopping traffic. Then use the three part sentence by saying something like, 'John, I can see you're keen to push this through; however, I need to be comfortable that it's the right decision, so I'd like to check the alternatives.' You can always back this up with the broken record.

Spurious logic

As our society is based on ancient Greek principles, we have all been taught to kowtow to logic. So anyone who uses logic, no matter how shaky its constituent parts, is bound to be right. Put simply, it is time to start thinking of logic as what other people use to prove you are wrong. There are two forms of spurious logic.

The first is where the other person *reduces your points to a ridiculous level*. I once observed a casual debate between friends about vegetarianism. The debate moved from factory farming methods to sanctity of life to the control of ants invading your house. The logical argument of the 'winner' was that if you don't mind killing ants, you don't believe in sanctity of life, so factory farming is not a problem, so vegetarianism is daft. In another debate someone commented that criminals get off too lightly and that courts ought to pass tougher sentences. The opposite case was taken up by another member of the group who quickly got everyone else agreeing that hanging people who double-park would be ridiculous. The first person's argument collapsed shortly afterwards.

The second form of spurious logic was used brilliantly in a recent detergent advert. The detergent manufacturer had invented soap tablets to replace powder. The tablets go in with the wash rather than in a soap drawer. There were two adverts, both featuring a young mother on the screen. A man, situated off-screen, is quizzing her about the new detergent tablets. His questions conclude with, 'So would you go back to using powder?' to which she responds, 'Would you go back to using an outside toilet?' We are given no technical information whatsoever about the superiority of tablets over powder but, if it's a choice of using the tablets or an outside toilet, I think we all know the answer. In the second advert, the mother has her young son with her, straight from a muddy soccer game. The off-screen questioner does his stuff once more and concludes with the comment, 'Surely, just being in tablet form can't make that much difference?' to which she replies, 'Oh yeah? And how many dirty soccer kits have you washed recently?' Again, we are given no technical information, but if the off-screen man's answer to her question is 'None', then he must be wrong and she must be right.

The logic is that *if a person is correct in one thing, they must be correct in the other thing.* The fact that the two things are completely unconnected never seems to dawn on us. Such is the power of logic.

You have only one defence against this form of manipulation – *in-depth probing*. You need to get to the bottom of the other person's point to see if the logic they are applying is sound or spurious. This also gives you the advantage of maximum thinking time. So your choice is simple. What would you rather do, take my advice or wash dirty soccer kits in an outside toilet? You choose.

Other forms of manipulation

You might like to be aware of some other forms of manipulation I have come across. You will find that being aware of them immensely reduces their impact on you.

Keeping you waiting

This is a tactic that senior people use on junior people and buyers use on sales representatives. It is a way of saying, 'I'm calling the tune around here because I'm the more important person.' Their hope is that you will either stew a little while you are waiting and so become more nervous or that the effect on your schedule will cause you to feel under pressure and so you will agree to what they want in order to keep the discussion short. An effective counter-measure, assuming you do not want to reschedule the meeting, is always to keep some work with you. (I keep a back-reading file in my briefcase containing magazine articles I have already scanned and want to read in more detail. This file, incidentally, also proves its worth when you are faced with delays in public transport, traffic jams, and so on.) That way, their attempt at pressure becomes a gift of time in which you did some work that you would not otherwise have done. Alternatively you can use the time for some last-minute preparation. I find it useful to do a last-minute mental dress rehearsal of the opening of the meeting or the handling of any particularly tricky bits. Finally, if the time available for the meeting becomes too squeezed you may have no alternative but to reschedule. If their delay was genuinely unavoidable, they will understand; if it was an attempt to manipulate you, they will see it has not worked and be less inclined to try it on you in the future.

The best offer

Picture the scene. The young sales rep enters Mr Big's office. He was up half the night ensuring that his sales pitch is word perfect. He is no more than 30 seconds into it when Mr Big's secretary comes through on the intercom with a pre-arranged message. 'Hello, Mr Big. Miss High-and-Mighty wants to see you in two minutes in her office.' What can Mr Big do, other than apologise and say, 'Well, let's skip the haggling. Just give me your best price.' He also lets slip, for good measure, that he has one of the sales rep's competitors coming in this afternoon. And what can the sales rep do but go straight to his fall-back price. Whether you are negotiating a price for a product, the start date for a project, or how many staff you can temporarily second to another department, watch out if the other party puts you under unexpected time pressure and attempts to push you straight to your fall-back position.

The sales rep could respond, 'I'd like to give you my best price but until I've learned more about your requirements, I don't know what my best price is.' At best that response will make Mr Big realise that pushing the sales rep is not the most sensible route to the best deal and, at the very least, it should let Mr Big know that he is not dealing with a push-over. Side-stepping the request and signalling that you need information is a good counter-measure. Interestingly, in this response, you have not disagreed with the other person. In fact you have done the reverse: you have agreed that you want to give them what they want. It is just that you cannot do it the way they have suggested.

The principal ploy

A favourite tactic in buying situations, the principal ploy, is also found in multidisciplinary project teams. In buying situations the sales rep is getting close to his fall-back position when he discovers that the person to whom he is talking does not have the authority to sign the order. The buyer leaves the room and returns five minutes later saying that his boss will not sign the order unless another x per cent discount is given. The buyer gets the x per cent, disappears again, and returns five minutes later saying that his boss wants delivery in two weeks instead of four. The unseen principal always wants a bit more. Sometimes only the threat of consulting a principal is enough. In management/union negotiations you will hear the phrase, 'My members will never agree to that' or 'The board of directors would never accept that.' In multidisciplinary teams, the accountant will have to check with the finance director, or the marketing manager will have to check with the marketing director on anything they do not like, and they will bring their 'principal's' demands to the discussion.

When the principal ploy is used against you, effective counter-measures are, first, to insist on discussing matters with the principal directly or, second, resurrect matters that the other party thought were already agreed. 'If you want delivery in two weeks and an x per cent discount we'll have to take another look at quantity.' That works just as well in non-sales situations. Furthermore, with this counter-measure you are not only side-stepping the attempted manipulation but also effectively encouraging the other person to be open and honest. That way you can arrive at an agreement with which you both feel comfortable.

The subsidiary decision

Here is an example. If you are unsure whether to buy a certain car or not, the sales person may ask you which colour you would prefer if you were to buy one. 'Red? Let me see if we have one in stock...Yes, I could have that ready for you tomorrow. Would you prefer delivery in the morning or the afternoon?' By asking you to make small decisions he is making the assumption that the big decision is already made. Waiver on a purchase decision in a shop and the sales assistant might ask, 'How do you prefer paying for items like this, cash or terms? – Terms? ... Let me see what the monthly repayments would be.' It is a pushy way of selling and it is a method of manipulation favoured by pushy people. 'I need to borrow one of your staff. Would you prefer to lend me Bill or Sally?' assumes that the decision whether to lend a member of staff at all has already been made. The only effective counter-measure is to keep your wits about you and remind them that the small decisions will be made only after the big decision. You are not refusing to help. It is just that you want to make the decision in your own way and in your own time. Use assertive language, good eye-contact and a neutral tone of voice and they will not try it on you again in a hurry. The effect is once more to teach them that if they want to influence you they will stand a better chance of doing so openly and positively rather than manipulatively.

These four manipulation tactics are most common in the sales world, although you will see them elsewhere. The remainder are more common outside sales situations.

Making you feel guilty or responsible

Let us say that a colleague wants a lift home. His car is being repaired and he does not want to miss his child's birthday party, which he probably will do if he uses public transport. You do not want to give him a lift because you want to be home in good time too. After several attempts to persuade you to agree, which you have resisted, he says, 'Well . . . because of you, I'll miss my little girl's birthday party. Boy, will she be upset.' People do this to each other all the

> time. You cannot let me have the figures when I want them so I'll miss my deadline. It is your fault. You cannot help me with something as I had hoped, which means that I will have to alter my plans. The inconvenience is your fault.

The best counter-measure is to think assertively and not to let other people make you feel guilty about standing up for your rights or to feel responsible for the predicament they have made for themselves. They may have a right to ask for your help but you may have a right to refuse it – without feeling guilty. The alternative is to allow other people to choose how you feel – and most of us would struggle in vain to see any sense in that!

Your personal defence shield

Probing and acknowledging have another, and significant, benefit when someone is trying to make you feel inadequate. They form a *barrier* between what the other person is saying and what you are feeling. That makes it easier for you to stay in control of your feelings and so behave by design rather than behave by default.

Assertiveness is one of those subjects that pervades all aspects of face-to-face communication. Most of us need to be more assertive. We spend too much time being either submissive or aggressive. Both these types of behaviour have more disadvantages than advantages because they are based on the sort of characteristics we do not like in people. Assertiveness, on the other hand, is based on the characteristics that we do value in others. When you think of the behavioural characteristics of your best-ever boss, colleague, subordinate, neighbour or friend, you are probably identifying assertiveness characteristics. The ability to be straight, open, and honest, combined with an ability to listen and to be tolerant with us when we fail to choose our words carefully, are characteristics we value in other people. It really does follow, therefore, that other people will value them in us too.

4

Core skill three
building rapport

Have you ever taken an instant like or dislike to someone? Have you ever been in discussion with someone and thought that they were just on a totally different wavelength or, alternatively, that they were totally in tune with you? Influencing is easier if the other person feels comfortable with you; if they feel they trust you; if they feel you understand them. That is what we mean by rapport. This chapter shows you how to use a variety of skills to remove unnecessary obstacles and, by using four behaviours, deliberately to create that feeling of trust and understanding.

Matching body language

If you watch two people in conversation who are getting on really well you will notice something about their body language. They tend to 'mirror' each other. They tend to sit or stand as if the one is a mirror image of the other. If they are eating or drinking they may even place food in their mouths or sip their drinks simultaneously. This body language matching happens unconsciously. It is a sign of rapport.

Conversely, if you watch two people in conversation who are not getting on well together, you will notice the opposite; the body language of one is different to the body language of the other. Before we go any further, a little bit of fine-tuning is necessary because you might be thinking, 'Well, I saw two people in an argument. They weren't getting on very well but their body language was very similar. They were in each other's face, shouting and jabbing fingers at each other.' They may not have been getting on very well but they were certainly on the same wavelength, albeit not a very productive one. At this stage, let us focus on more everyday situations.

There is you, and one other person whom you are trying to influence. Making your body language similar to theirs will make them feel more comfortable with you and improve your chances of success. Here is an example. On courses, I have put people into pairs and asked one of them to talk about a topic on which they hold strong, even emotional views. I have asked the other person to listen actively but to make their posture different from their partner. After a couple of minutes I have interrupted their discussion and asked the listener now to adopt a more similar posture. After another couple of minutes, I have reconvened them and asked the 'talker' to describe their feelings about the 'listener'. The result is invariable. They say things like, 'In the first half of the conversation, I wasn't getting through to them but, in the second half, they were beginning to see things my way', or 'In the first half they just weren't listening but in the second half they paid much more attention'. When you consider that they know it is an exercise to demonstrate 'something' and that they have heard the instructions about posture given to their partner, I feel that the consistency of response proves the point. People feel more comfortable with you when you mirror their body language. But please note the word is 'mirror' not 'mimic'. If you mimic their body language they will think you are making fun of them!

Pacing thinking

Before I explain pacing thinking, read the following dialogue between two work colleagues, Jim and Sally. Jim has just been offered a promotion and is telling Sally about it. When you have finished, ask yourself what you have learned about Jim.

Sally	*Will you take it?*
Jim	It's a very attractive offer.
Sally	*What do you like about it?*
Jim	The opportunity. It's a real challenge. It would look great on my CV.
Sally	*It's a tough job as well as an important one. How do you feel it would enhance your CV?*
Jim	It isn't just a promotion. It means changing the culture of the whole depot. That would prepare me for bigger and better things. I can't get that experience anywhere else in the organisation.
Sally	*Bigger and better things sound important to you.*
Jim	There's nothing wrong with being ambitious. I'll just have to sell the move to Nancy and the kids.
Sally	*You feel they'll need persuading?*
Jim	They're very settled and very happy here.

	But you've got to take the long-term view, haven't you?
Sally	*Long-term thinking can be important. You're looking to the future then?*
Jim	Of course, I don't want to be stuck in this role for the next 20 years. I'd be bored silly. I'd wind up like my father, for crying out loud.
Sally	*Why is not winding up like your dad so important?*
Jim	He spent most of his life doing the same boring job because it was the loyal thing to do. Then he got made redundant and the shock made him ill. He didn't last long after that.
Sally	*When you think back to those times, how do you feel?*
Jim	Very resentful. Companies shouldn't treat people like that and, anyway, he should have kept his eye on the ball a bit more, then he'd have seen it coming.

So, what have you just learned about Jim? Many people feel he is very ambitious which stems from an unpleasant childhood experience. They also feel his ambition is self-ish and could cause domestic problems. By comparison, if you ask yourself what you have just learned about Sally, the answer is 'nothing' – and that, I want to emphasise strongly, is very important *and very unusual.*

Why is it important? This promotion issue is very impor-tant to Jim. At this stage of the conversation, the best thing Sally can do is *listen*, but to do so in a way that *keeps pace* with Jim's thinking. The better the rapport between Jim and Sally at this stage of the conversation, the better the chances of Sally influencing Jim's thinking later on. So please notice that all Sally does in the conversation is to ask Jim questions about what he has just said, or she summarises or she reflects Jim's words back to him. Jim feels comfortable talking to Sally.

Why is it unusual? I will bet that as you were reading the dialogue you wanted to tell Jim something. Maybe that he was absolutely correct and he ought to go for it or that he ought to think twice before dragging his family to the other end of the country. Or maybe the conversation reminded you of something that happened to you once, or to someone you know. Let's explore both these issues using a fictitious situation as an example.

The rush to judge

Where a friend anxiously tells you that he has accrued large credit card debts, there are, according to psychologist Carl Rogers, *five typical responses*:

1 Well, that's just irresponsible.
2 That's because you've got no willpower.
3 Oh, it's really easy to spend more than you can afford when you've got credit cards. It's happened to me too.
4 How much in debt are you?
5 The debts are more than you're comfortable with?

These responses are, in turn, judging, interpreting, sympathising, exploring, and reflecting. Because most of us have a tendency to judge or interpret, these two responses are the most common. They are also the least helpful to rapport. The least common responses are exploring and reflecting, yet they are most helpful to rapport because when someone is anxious, as in this example, they need to feel that we are *listening on the same wavelength*.

The recognition machine

Our brains are very efficient recognition machines. For example, an actor you have seen on television may be in a drama requiring heavy make-up and period costume, yet there is something about the eyes, the voice or a gesture that you recognise. Our brains perform the same 'recognition' trick with situations. They pick up a few features of a situation and check to see what kind of situation it is. It is part of our learning process, and removes the necessity to re-learn every situation from scratch. That is very useful. It can, however, present a problem when rapport is important, because when someone says something to us we quickly flick through our mental data banks and 'recognise' the situation.

Many of us seem to have a 'hot line' from this recognition process straight to our vocal chords. So in the credit card example, our response would be, 'Oh, that happened to me once. Let me tell you all about it.' Or in the promotion example, Sally could have responded, 'Jim, I know someone who was in exactly the same position and it didn't work out at all well. What happened to them was...' All you will have succeeded in doing is breaking rapport because, in both examples, the other person needs to be listened to. You need to pace their thinking, not vocalise your own.

This can even happen in ordinary conversation when someone is telling you something that is important to them. It is their limelight. If you rush to judge, or if you recognise and let the hot line take over, you will break rapport. So, in situations where it is important for influencing that you maintain rapport, pace their thinking for that part of the conversation.

Signposting

This 'recognition' trick of our brains can lead to another problem. It has happened to most of us. We say something to someone and the other person misinterprets our meaning. We think we are making a helpful point, for example, and they 'hear' a disagreement. At best, we do not get their full attention because part of their thinking is categorising what we are saying. (Remember 'integration' from the communication process?) By 'signposting', we can get their full attention and reduce the likelihood of their misunderstanding what we are saying.

You probably do some signposting already. Most people do. Every time you say, 'On the one hand...' the other person knows that you are about to present two sides to something because your next sentence will almost certainly begin, 'But on the other hand...'. When you begin a sentence, 'In conclusion...' you are signposting that this is your last point. Signposting helps keep the other person on your wavelength, so my advice is that you do it more often. Signposts like those listed below help rapport by getting the other person's attention and helping them categorise what you are saying:

> Let me play devil's advocate for a moment. What would happen if...
> Here's an example. When I was...
> Let's take a hypothetical situation. If we...
> Let me check my understanding. What you seem to be saying is...

Signposting works in both simple and complex situations. Imagine you have been promoted to run a section 'over the head' of a member of staff who thought they were the heir apparent. The member of staff then appears resentful and uncooperative towards you. You want to discuss this highly sensitive matter with them but, understandably, you might be unsure how to open the conversation, and are reluctant to appear either too confrontational or too soft. Depending on the exact circumstances, you might try this: at the end of a routine meeting with the person put down your pen, close the file, or do something to signal that that part of the discussion is over. Then say calmly, in a neutral tone of voice:

> There's something I'd like to discuss with you. It's a bit sensitive so may I just describe how it looks to me?

The member of staff will know that the conversation is about to take a different direction; that it is a sensitive matter; and that you are going to describe something from your point of view, which implies that you are going to make neither judgements nor accusations. You have also requested their permission to describe it, which signals that you respect them. It is also an easy few words to remember and practise so that they can be delivered fluently. You are therefore less likely to deliver them too abruptly or too submissively. That's signposting.

The signposting exception

There is, however, one exception to the rule. If you signpost that you are about to disagree you will break rapport. So even though you are being honest, your behaviour is leading to an outcome you probably do not want. Even if you follow quickly with your perfectly valid reasons, it will be too late. To maintain rapport, describe no more than one or two compelling reasons and then explain that, for those reasons, you would like to discuss alternatives.

Rapport breakers and rapport builders

Imagine trying very hard to influence someone, only to fail and then, to add insult to injury, to discover that you caused them to disagree by inadvertently breaking rapport when you needed it most. When trying to influence someone, we often use behaviours that we feel strengthen our case. Far from building rapport, however, many of these behaviours actually break it. Here is a list of rapport breakers together with suggested replacements that build rapport.

Talking more than listening

There are two reasons why this is unproductive. First, anyone who talks more than they listen discovers less about the other person. They understand less about their situation, their priorities, the constraints within which they have to work, and so on. They understand less about what the other person will buy and so understand less how to sell their product or idea to them. Second, when someone tries to dominate an influencing situation, they are usually trying to manipulate. So at worst they are resorting to trickery, and at best they are a bore. Even in social situations, where influencing might be the last thing on someone's mind, we rarely warm to people who dominate a conversation (unless they happen to be exceedingly entertaining). So *listen more than talk*. Use your words sparingly but deliberately.

Using 'formalspeak'

In everyday conversations, if someone starts speaking 'formally' it drives a wedge between us and breaks rapport. Formalspeak can be subtle:

> At this moment in time
> In the fullness of time
> Ongoing
> It has been brought to my attention that…

Would you use phraseology like that in normal conversations? No: you would say 'Now', 'Eventually', 'Continuing' and 'I understand that…'. Even using the full form of words can sound formal. In everyday conversation we say 'I'll' instead of 'I will', 'you'd' instead of 'you would' and 'can't' instead of 'cannot'. As soon as someone starts using the full form of these words, especially if accompanied by a 'stiffening' of body language, it is usually a sign that rapport is breaking down. So, be aware of the kind of language the other person is using and, if you spot it, start pacing and probing. Avoid such language yourself; *use everyday language.*

Parental language

When adults speak to children, they often speak autocratically. 'You *must* remember...', 'You *ought* to...', 'You *can't*...', 'You *should*...'. Children do not like it when an adult speaks to them like this (but they cannot do much about it because we are bigger than they are). When one adult speaks to another adult this way, however, the other adult positively detests it. The reason for this reaction is because of the underlying assumptions.

Adults assume they are superior to children. They assume they have to make decisions on the child's behalf. They assume they have to impose rules on the child or compensate for the child's inadequacies by looking after them. The terminology sends a small but unmistakable signal of how the speaker is feeling, and that signal is picked up by the other person. Rapport beaks down. So when an adult uses this terminology to us, we resent the underlying assumptions and react negatively. Bearing in mind the above examples, you might get a better response if you say, 'Please remember...', 'How would you feel if I suggested...?', 'I'd prefer you not to...', Have you tried...?' So *use adult-to-adult language.*

Irritators

We often use some words and phrases in the mistaken belief that they boost our case when, in truth, they irritate the other person to such an extent that they break rapport and so weaken our case. When someone says 'With respect . . .' we feel we are about to be insulted. (If they begin the sentence 'With all *due* respect . . .' it is an odds-on certainty!) Similarly 'I hear what you say, but . . .' usually means that they have no intention of listening to us. Even words such as 'generous', 'fair' and 'reasonable' can backfire on us. If we say, 'This is a very generous offer' or, 'I'm being very reasonable about this', we are breaking rapport because if the other person thought our offer generous or reasonable they would have snapped it up. So these words only serve to emphasise the distance between us.

Other irritators include phrases like, 'Let's be honest' or 'Let's be reasonable' because you are effectively accusing the other person of deluding themselves or being unreasonable. Even repeated use of the word 'obviously' has potential to irritate. 'Obviously everyone understands this point' or 'Obviously we can't pay that much' are redundant sentences. If everyone really does understand the point or already knows that you cannot pay that much there is no need to say it. If, on the other hand, they do not know, you have just irritated them or possibly even insulted them.

Another irritator is persistent use of the 'royal *we*'. While there are situations when you can and should use 'we', such as when representing your organisation or when talking about a collective response, if you are simply trying to add weight to your argument by saying 'we' instead of 'I' it always sounds wrong. Appraisal discussions are a good example. I sometimes hear appraising managers say,

'We feel that you aren't quite ready for promotion' or, 'We felt that you hadn't quite grasped the importance of that part of the project.' The effect of the 'royal we' is always the same. First, it drives a wedge between the two people because it is effectively saying, 'I am a chief and you are an indian so don't try to disagree with me.' Second, it sets off a thought process in the other person's mind; if you have to hide behind the corporate 'we' then either your case must be very weak indeed or you lack the courage of your convictions. For example, people hide behind the 'royal we' when they do not want to do something. 'We couldn't possibly agree to that' usually means 'I'd have to take a decision by myself. That means sticking my neck out. I'd rather not.' So *show respect* when influencing, and avoid such irritators.

Doing their thinking for them

Unless you are telepathic, you do not know what is going on in someone else's mind, so any statements that suggest you do are liable to irritate them. Every time you promote your case by saying, 'What you don't seem to realise is . . .' or 'What you have clearly forgotten is . . .', you antagonise the other person and break rapport. Far better to ask them, 'What are you basing that statement on?' or 'Can I just check, what part . . . played in your thinking.' That way you stand a better chance of getting them to rethink their position. So *probe rather than assume.*

Being dogmatic

You may already be aware that behaviour from one person can trigger off a response from another. According to research by Peter Honey and colleagues, there is a high degree of consistency in triggers and responses. In round figures, being dogmatic about something, such as when presenting your idea as a strong statement ('Listen, we've got to...'), produces a 60 per cent chance that the other person will disagree with you. If, on the other hand, you present exactly the same idea as a question ('How would you feel if I suggested...?' or 'How do you think people would react if we...?') there is a 60 per cent chance that the other person will agree or even build on your idea. So rather than trying to bulldoze your ideas through or presenting people with faits accomplis, *suggest* and *encourage them to consider* your suggestions.

Making counter-proposals

The worst time to make a proposal is when the other person is wondering why we are not considering theirs. There are two reasons why we fall into this trap. The first is that we genuinely do not like their proposal and so we deliver our own. The second is that their proposal triggers a good idea in our minds that we blurt out. Either way, we are on a different wavelength from the other person. They are mentally geared up to discuss their proposal. No matter how good our proposal, we are attempting to sow it on stony ground. The conversation can even degenerate into a kind of verbal ping-pong. It is far better to discuss their proposal. Ask questions about it to *encourage them to think it through* and to signal that you do not readily accept it, then present your proposal in the form of a suggestion.

Facilitating defend/attack spirals

When we human beings are attacked we tend to react either by being very defensive or by counter-attacking. It is a natural human trait. It also causes problems when trying to influence someone. The first problem is that, because it is a natural human trait, it tends to be reciprocated: they attack, you defend. Your defence comes across as a counter-attack and so they have to respond appropriately. The second problem is that even a denial of an allegation can be seen as a counter-attack. Either way, before you know where you are, you are in a defend/attack spiral – downwards! The only workable course of action is to *be totally solution-oriented*. So even if an allegation is made against you, it will be sensible to respond only briefly and to move on quickly towards a solution without waiting for a counter-response.

Something subtle

Here are two more influencing skills you might like to think about when building rapport. They come from the increasingly popular subject of neuro-linguistic programming (NLP for short). To illustrate the first one, here are two alternative ways in which a trainer might open a course on appraisal skills for managers who are unwilling delegates. The managers have not got time for appraisal and think it is a lot of nonsense designed to keep the personnel department busy. The trainer needs to get their attention, and maybe even intrigue them, in the first few opening remarks. Read both openings and decide which you think will build most rapport with them.

Opening 1

Good morning. A lot of managers neglect their responsibilities by failing to give sufficient priority to staff appraisal. What they don't seem to realise is that the performance of their staff and *their* performance are the same thing. So, I'm sure you'll agree with me when I say that time spent developing staff is always time well spent. Far too many managers allow their staff to perform below their full potential so I'm going to show you how to use appraisal to improve staff performance to the benefit of them, yourself and the organisation. Let's begin.

Opening 2

Good morning. You probably already know that *staff* performance tends to reflect on a *manager*'s performance. So, eventually, most managers come to realise that time spent developing the performance of their staff benefits themselves too. I could tell you that, right now, your staff might have untapped performance potential, but you probably already know that. I'm wondering if you'll grasp the opportunities available in this course to tap into that potential. Can you imagine the effect on performance, motivation and your reputation as a manager when, as a result of what you learn today, you help each team member develop their skills? Let's begin.

In reading these two openings, you might even have imagined a tone of voice accompanying each one. Accompanying the first opening, people often imagine a superior, dry or condescending tone of voice, because that is how the words come across to them. Accompanying the second opening, they often imagine a warmer, inviting and respectful tone of voice because they find these words have a comfortable feel to them. While in the second opening, I avoided some of the 'irritators' present in the first, I also included *embedded suggestions*.

Embedded suggestions are suggestions that, if spoken on their own, would sound like orders (and, in this context, orders would certainly alienate the course delegates). Instead, the suggestions are 'embedded' in other phrases. It is this embedding process that makes them easy to hear. For your ease of reference, I have shown the suggestions and embedding phrases below.

Embedding phrases	Suggestions
You probably already know that...	*staff* performance reflects on a *manager*'s performance
Eventually, most managers come to realise that...	time spent developing the performance of their staff benefits themselves too
I could tell you that...but you probably already know	right now, your staff might have untapped performance potential
I'm wondering if you'll...	grasp the opportunities available in this course
Can you imagine the [benefits]...	when you help each team member develop their skills

As you mentally rehearse something you want to say to someone, you might like to try embedding a few suggestions in phrases like those above. You can think of the suggestions you want to make to the other person and then choose some appropriate embedding phrases. You might find that what you say feels different, that it has a gentler, more inviting tone to it. To help you feel comfortable with embedded suggestions, you can practise in social situations before you try them out in more formal settings. Eventually, you will feel more comfortable with these phrases and they will come more naturally to you. If you want to, you can even go back over this paragraph and identify the suggestions I have embedded in it for you.

The second influencing skill is based on the fact that our experiences register on us in different ways. Some people 'see' experiences, others 'hear' them, and others 'feel' them. People give clues as to how their experiences register by using relevant terminology in their conversation. 'That looks fine', 'That sounds great' and 'That feels good to me' are all ways of saying the same thing, but each statement indicates the way the speakers register their experiences in different ways – visually, auditorily and kinetically. You can use this information to help build rapport. Here is an example:

Jean   So that's what our department has been asked to do. What do you think?

Bill   If I'm honest, Jean, it doesn't *sound* too good to me. I'd like to *hear* something more relevant to us.

Sam	From my point of *view*, it doesn't *look* too good either. I just can't *see* what's wrong with the way we're handling this issue right now.
Jean	OK. I had a long conversation with head office, and I can tell you I was sceptical too, yet they managed to convince me. Let me run through their arguments. As I do, Bill, you might want to *listen* for anything that *rings a bell* from the project we worked on last year and, Sam, *look* at the statistics and I'm sure you'll *see* the relevance.

These are the many behaviours you can use deliberately to encourage a feeling of rapport – that feeling of comfort and confidence that makes influencing so much easier. You might like to flick through the pages again to home in on those behaviours you could usefully practise to make influencing easier for yourself.

5

Core skill four
influencing groups

Everything we have looked at so far, persuasive probing, being assertive and building rapport, is as relevant to influencing groups as it is to influencing individuals. With groups, however, there is more to consider because, as there are more people involved, the propensity for problems is greater. So if you find yourself on committees, in meetings, going before interview panels and so on, the following guide will help you influence groups better.

Co-ordinate the group's wavelength

Imagine being in a meeting where someone makes a suggestion. The suggestion may be imperfect but it has a few good points going for it. People in the meeting react in different ways. One person spots the potential in the suggestion and tries to build on it. Another spots a flaw in the suggestion and tries to point out the problems. Another focuses on costs or other facts, such as time-scale, staff requirements, facilities needed, etc. Another does not like the idea for emotional reasons, pointing out that it looks like change for the sake of it or that staff will not like the shift in values that the suggestion embraces. They are all talking about the same suggestion and *they are all making valid points.* As they are all approaching the suggestion from different angles, however, they are on different wavelengths and the propensity for misunderstanding and disagreement is immense. There is nothing wrong with anyone's input to the discussion. The problem is in the lack of co-ordination and sequencing. A bit like with an orchestra in which everyone is playing the right notes but at a time that suits them individually. The music sounds dreadful. This is how many good ideas are lost. It could be yours!

Imagine the difference, however, if someone suggested that everyone involved in the discussion proceeded in an orderly fashion. For example they could say,

> OK, Jean has just come up with a suggestion. Let's spend the next few minutes talking about it. First, let's build on it and see if we can knock it into some sort of shape. Next, we'll talk facts. See how much it might cost, what staff requirements and facilities it might take. Then we'll all do some negative thinking, see what problems we can identify. Finally, we'll all talk openly, describing how we feel about the suggestion. Who'd like to go first?

Adopting this sort of approach helps to get everyone approaching the suggestion from the same angle.

So, whenever a group discussion flounders it is worth asking yourself whether it is because people are on different wavelengths and, if so, suggesting that you all co-ordinate your thinking. If someone proposes an idea, the next most productive action to take might be to develop it; if someone makes a statement that triggers people's emotions the next most productive action might be to discuss openly how everyone feels about it.

Most of us would like to think that a chairperson would take on this role and manage the process of the discussion. In reality they often have either too much of a stake in the outcome of the discussion, or are too busy gathering information, to be efficient at observing the process. Not to mention the fact that they just might be the most senior person there, so others defer to their status.

It is my experience, however, that the person who influences the *process of the discussion* manages to influence the *decisions* that are taken. So your input might be to make comments such as

> We seem to be getting bogged down in costs on this one, yet we haven't determined what the benefits could be.

> John, I can see you're very keen on this idea: you're pushing it very hard. But a moment ago everyone agreed that you would all generate as many alternatives as possible. I feel as if your persistence is hindering the generation of other ideas.

> It seems as if the discussion has lost some momentum. Would it help if I summarised the main arguments for and against, and then perhaps we could take a decision?

If necessary, you can make these suggestions through the chairperson. The effect will be the same, however; in influencing the process, you are influencing the decisions.

So watch out for different 'angles of approach' putting people on different wavelengths. The main ones you will see are:

- creative, when people are trying to generate alternatives or build on someone else's idea
- negative, when people are spotting problems or exceptions
- pragmatic/factual, when people are considering facts like costs, resources, time-scales, and so on
- emotional, when people are considering feelings
- detail, when people are thinking about small parts of the idea or its application
- overview, when people are thinking about all of the idea or its application.

If you are aware of 'where they are coming from' you will understand them better. If you signpost where you are coming from, they will understand you better.

The right behaviours

In addition to co-ordinating the group's wavelength you can also check to see if your behaviours are having a positive or negative effect on the group. I have listed them below under four headings:

- *Goal*, because if everyone shares a common understanding of what the group is to achieve you not only have a better chance of achieving it, you can 'refocus' anyone who wants to go off at a tangent

- *Process*, because if everyone understands how the goal is to be achieved, the discussion becomes co-ordinated
- *Understanding*, because, in group discussions, some people fight their corner very strongly, others are there to represent their section, and some have a mandate from their boss. So understanding why they are adopting a particular line or what their priorities are always helps
- *Cohesion*, because some people like to dominate a group discussion; others feel more secure if they say nothing and others like to start break-away discussions. The person who keeps the group together, understanding one another and following the agreed process to achieve the commonly understood goal, usually manages to influence the decisions. They do so because they have established their credibility and because others in the group listen to the points they make.

	Unhelpful behaviours	Helpful behaviours
Goal and Process	No goal or process	Suggesting goal or process
	Conflicting goals	Referring back to goal
	Ignoring goal	or process
Understanding	Excessive talking	Probing, seeking information
	Being dogmatic	Clarifying
	Not listening	Listening
	Disagreeing	Building on others' suggestions
	Being negative	Signposting
	Changing wave-length without signposting	Suggesting alternatives for consideration
Cohesion	Ignoring or losing people's input	Inviting contributions
	Dominating the discussion	Co-ordinating thinking modes
	Not participating	Summarising input so far
	Starting or joining a break-away discussion	Relating input to goal or process
		Suggesting decisions

So, when it comes to influencing groups, the bottom line is if you influence the *process of the discussion* you are more likely to influence the *decisions* that are taken.

6

Understanding body language

While you have been reading the dialogues in previous chapters, you might have been imagining an accompanying tone of voice, facial expression and gestures. Body language is relevant to all four core skills. Consequently, rather than include a section in each chapter, I have provided the essentials for you here.

Why is body language so important?

Body language is the phrase used to describe the thousands of messages we transmit with our bodies rather than with our words. It is important for two main reasons.

■ Most people are unaware of their body language so it comes out unedited. By observing someone's body language, therefore, you can learn a lot about what they are thinking and how they are feeling.

■ Unless you control your body language, it too will come out unedited and other people will learn a lot about what you are thinking and feeling! Consequently, you need to control it. This is partly to ensure that it supports, rather than contradicts, what you are saying and partly because, with some gentle 'stage management', you can boost your influencing skills.

Many people are intrigued by the concept of body language. They wonder how it is possible to tell so much from such small and seemingly innocent gestures. Here is an example. When someone is lying, they are often in a state of heightened anxiety because they are afraid of being found out. According to some specialists, this heightened state of anxiety causes increased blood flow in the nasal passages. This creates a strange sensation in the liar's nose which he or she relieves subconsciously with more frequent 'hand to nose' gestures. Some people then draw the conclusion that touching one's nose is a sign of lying and they wonder what other 'secrets' of body language are waiting to be discovered. I like to remind people of four keys to understanding body language that will help their positive influencing skills.

The four keys to understanding body language

Raise your awareness

Body language was the first language you learned, so you probably already know sufficient about it. All you have to do is increase your awareness. If you are unsure about that statement, ask yourself how you would know whether someone was happy, sad, anxious, confident, feeling uncomfortable with your proposal, or openly concerned that more details have still to be finalised. Think about it, and you will describe a range of non-verbal signals. You will probably begin with obvious ones such as a smile or droopy eyes, a worried expression and a frown, a shift in posture or direct eye contact.

The more you think about it, however, the more you will start to describe subtle non-verbal signals such as evasive eyes, a tightening of the lips or using an arm to 'protect' the stomach. In real situations you will even find that you will spot and correctly interpret signals of which you were not even consciously aware, such as increased dilation of someone's pupils!

Look for clusters and timing

Subtle, individual gestures are rarely as important as *clusters* of behaviours and the *timing* of changes. The former are important because in a cluster there are lots of gestures all transmitting (and therefore confirming) the same message. The latter are important because they usually occur in response to an inner reaction of some sort.

Here is an example. Imagine you are conducting a selection interview. As the candidate is telling you about how he successfully restructured part of his organisation he leans back in his chair, is inclined to one side, gesticulates naturally with one hand while the elbow of the other rests on the arm of the chair. His legs are crossed openly (the ankle of one leg resting on the knee of the other), his mouth is in a permanent smile while he talks, and his voice is firm and clear. Judging by this cluster of behaviours, how would you say he feels? Probably, very relaxed and confident.

Imagine that you then ask him a question probing his role in this restructuring. He still leans back in his chair but sits more upright. He clasps both hands together, one arm still resting on that of the chair but the other now pulled tightly across his stomach. His legs change from an open cross to a closed one (the back of one knee resting on top of the other knee). His smile begins to flicker, and his voice becomes more hesitant as he searches for the words to answer. Judging by this new cluster of behaviour, how would you say he feels now? Probably, distinctly nervous. And what would you say about the timing of the change? Your question about his role in the restructuring must have touched a nerve and, if his experience in restructuring is material to the assessment process, the matter should be probed in more detail.

Look for congruency

When body language supports what someone is saying we call it 'congruent'. Let's say you make a suggestion to someone and then ask how they feel about it. If they say, 'Fine' while looking you in the eye, smiling and nodding, you can probably believe them. Because people tend to think more about the words they speak than what they say with their bodies, their body language will sometimes send a contradictory message. This time when they say, 'Fine', you notice that their lips have tightened, a slight frown has developed and they are glancing down and away from you. You might assume that they are not happy with your suggestion despite what they say.

Think culture

Certain aspects of body language are universally recognised. A smile is the best example. It is recognised in every culture. Many aspects of body language, however, do not translate from one culture to another. If you stand directly facing someone with your arms folded across your chest while making direct eye contact with them you are exhibiting what, in many cultures, would be a sign of challenge or aggression. In Vietnam, however, that stance would be a sign of respect. If someone avoids eye contact with you, you may feel that they are being either evasive or very submissive. In Japan they may just be showing deference to you. And if you want real confusion, try disagreeing with someone from southern India by shaking your head. They will be delighted that you have just agreed with them! The summary that follows therefore applies mostly to North Europeans and North Americans.

Body language signals to watch for

▧ *Eyes*. The eyes can transmit a variety of messages. Looking directly at someone can signal interest, confidence, or aggression. When we are nervous, emotionally uncomfortable or submissive we often avert our eyes downwards and away from the other person. It is, however, worth avoiding total and persistent eye contact, especially when talking to a submissive person, because it can be intimidating. Eye contact between 50 and 70 per cent of the time is enough to make people feel that you are attentive. And if you always accompany a serious point with eye contact you will stand a much better chance of being taken seriously.

Tone of voice. Think of tone of voice as being made up of the emphasis we place on different words, the pitch of the sound, the volume of our speech and its speed. People infer a lot from tone of voice. When we are cool, calm and collected all the ingredients are moderate. The emphasis we place on various words serves to help the communication process. Emphasis is usually on factual words rather than on personal or emotive ones. Our pitch is comfortable. We speak neither too loudly nor too softly, and our speed of speech has just the right pace in it.

When we become angry, however, all that changes. We emphasise emotive words; the pitch of our voice usually goes lower, while volume and pace increase. When we are feeling nervous our voice becomes quieter, pitch and speed often increase and we emphasise conciliatory, apologetic and sympathy-seeking words. We also tend to ramble, speaking far more than we need to, as if we know that conflict may arise when we finish speaking and so we try to put it off as long as possible by going on and on.

To display confidence in your case, therefore, you need a neutral tone of voice. Emphasis has to go on factual words; pitch, volume and speed all have to be relatively neutral. Posture helps greatly with tone of voice, so that is what we shall look at next.

Posture. **Posture** can signify a lot about the way we feel. When feeling vulnerable we tend to 'close up' just as if we were protecting ourselves physically. The main part of our body that we protect is the abdomen. A typical action might be to fold our arms tightly across the stomach or to put one arm across the stomach in a quasi-relaxed posture. Many people do, of course, sit with their arms folded or with an arm across their bodies quite comfortably and signify nothing by it.

So remember, we are looking for clusters of behaviour and part of the cluster we would look for is the tightness of the arms across the stomach, and their height. In a closed, protective posture they tend to be lower than in a relaxed posture. We also tend, when feeling vulnerable, to cross our legs knee to knee rather than ankle to knee. In an attempt to make ourselves appear smaller we 'shrink' a little, lowering the shoulders and curling the torso.

When feeling aggressive we do the opposite, and attempt to appear bigger. Whether standing or sitting we stretch up with our backs and puff out our chests (sometimes exaggerating the size of our chests by folding our arms high across them). We also tend to hold ourselves relatively rigid, which means that, once puffed out, the chest tends to stay that way, interfering with inhalation and exhalation.

In considering what type of posture is best for influencing, you need to consider what type of influencing situation you are in. Is it formal or informal? In most situations it will look better if you stick more to the informal, partly because you will look more relaxed and hence confident in your position, and partly because it is more likely to be appropriate. Unless an influencing situation is very serious or highly procedural, looking confidently relaxed will add to your credibility. It tends to be people who are unsure of their position, or nervous of their ability, who need the 'security blanket' of formality when it is not relevant. In seeking the support of unnecessary formality they undermine their own credibility.

- *Proximity.* We tend to be comfortable with a certain amount of space around us and we feel uncomfortable if someone else 'invades' it. The amount of space we feel is ours depends on two things: first, the situation we are in, and second, what we are used to.

  As for situation, we each have several 'zones' around us. The farthest away is the *public zone*. It is about 3.5 metres away from us and it is the distance we like to be from a large group of people we are addressing. Closer than that, in such a situtation, and we feel uncomfortable.

  Next comes the *social zone*, extending from about 1 to 3.5 metres from us. This is the distance we like to keep people we do not know very well, such as the gas repairman, a shop assistant, a new employee, and so on.

Next comes the *personal zone*, which extends from about 50 centimetres to 1 metre. This is the distance at which we feel comfortable at social and friendly gatherings.

Next comes the *intimate zone*, which extends from 15 to 50 centimetres. It is by far the most important to us. We guard it closely and feel very uncomfortable or even threatened if someone unwelcome enters it. It is usually reserved for lovers, parents, spouse, children, and very close friends and relatives.

From 0 to 15 centimetres there is a *close intimate zone* which can only really be entered during physical contact.

What we are used to plays a part within these overall guidelines. Someone brought up in a crowded city will feel comfortable with smaller zones than someone brought up in a sparsely populated rural area.

While the concept of zones does not apply in some situations, such as on crowded public transport, if we are to be comfortable with other people, and they with us, we need to stay within the appropriate zone. If you are too far away for a given set of circumstances you will appear ill at ease. If you are too close you will make the other person nervous. I have seen people giving sales presentations or presentations to senior managers fail to establish the right rapport with their audience because they have tried to get too close. I have seen interviewers make interviewees feel nervous because they have placed the interviewee's chair in the public rather than the social zone. I have seen people who, when welcoming new employees, have tried to be friendly and put an arm around their shoulder – only to make them feel uncomfortable.

- *Gestures.* As with other aspects of body language, it is possible to send positive and negative signals with your gestures, and also to assess how someone else is receiving you by the gestures they make. So here we shall look at the main categories of gestures.

We show anxiety in relation to another person by protecting ourselves with, say, folded arms but often we hug or hang on to our arms at the same time. We can achieve the same feeling of security by hugging a file or a bag close to our chest. Anxiety, especially when we feel threatened, causes our palms to sweat which we remove by rubbing them together as if we were washing them.

Anger and aggression cause us to 'attack' the other person with our forefinger, either by shaking it at them or by jabbing it in their direction. Sometimes, when we disagree with something, we erect a physical barrier by folding our arms between us and the other person. This would probably be accompanied by a slight backwards and upwards movement of the head.

When we are listening to someone and considering what they are saying we often put a hand up to our cheek or our chin. The hand in no way supports our head, however, as that is an obvious sign of boredom. When we wish to indicate sincerity we frequently show people the palms of our hands. (If you are not sure about this one, stand in front of a mirror and 'sell' yourself a second-hand car, saying, 'And it's only had one careful lady owner.') Unfortunately this is a gesture that is overused by everyone from politicians to second-hand-car salespeople when trying to convince us of something. But in everyday situations you should be safe with this gesture, if used sparingly.

When we disapprove of something but feel constrained about saying so, we often exhibit *displacement activity*, such as turning our face away from the speaker and picking imaginary lint from our clothes. A speaker who is not tuned in to body language would pass over this signal, but one who is alert would invite the lint-picker to share their thoughts.

When we are talking to someone and feel both superior and confident we often 'steeple' our fingers. It is a gesture common among managers and professionals such as accountants and lawyers when giving advice to clients or staff.

A vital point to remember is that most of the information that reaches our brain enters via the sense of sight. We pick up and process visual information very rapidly indeed, often without knowing that we have done so. Where there is a contradiction between what someone is telling us with their words and what they are inadvertently telling us with their body language it is the latter that we pay attention to every time.

So, by paying attention to eye contact, tone of voice, posture, proximity, and hand gestures we can not only reinforce our spoken words but we can also minimise the chances of inadvertently antagonising other people. By observing other people's body language we can assess how our words are being received, and determine how best to approach those people.

Pause for thought

Before we move on, you may like to pause for thought and consider to what extent you currently use the core skills. Try the questionnaire opposite.

When trying to influence someone, how often do you:
(tick the appropriate box)

		Rarely	Sometimes	Often
1	talk more than you listen?	☐	☐	☐
2	feel that the other person is talking about things that you feel are irrelevant?	☐	☐	☐
3	feel that your understanding and that of the other person are getting further apart rather than closer together?	☐	☐	☐
4	share with the other person what you are thinking or feeling?	☐	☐	☐
5	genuinely seek to understand the other person so that you can present your case in terms they will appreciate?	☐	☐	☐
6	consciously manage your own body language and observe that of the other person?	☐	☐	☐
7	make assumptions from one isolated gesture or movement?	☐	☐	☐
8	find that your behaviour is more of a response to your emotions rather than a considered action leading towards a positive outcome?	☐	☐	☐
9	help other people to speak up for themselves even if you disagree with them?	☐	☐	☐
10	feel that you have been pushed, coerced, or tricked into doing something?	☐	☐	☐

7

Gameplans

Here is an analogy: within reason, a cook could use a cupboard-full of ingredients to produce a variety of different meals by using them in different quantities and cooking them in different ways. So we can use our core skills for a variety of different situations by using them in different quantities and in different ways. This chapter shows how to do that by presenting a selection of 'gameplans' aimed at a variety of situations that people sometimes find difficult.

A *gameplan* is a set of tactics or the 'strategy' that can be adopted for a given situation. The situations covered will include those that people on my courses refer to as the most common or most troublesome. As the nature of each situation varies so does the format of the following sections. Some are more prescriptive than others, and some are more detailed than others. You can use the gameplans to improve your general knowledge of influencing skills or as a source of reference. The gameplans cover the following issues:

- appraisals and giving performance feedback
- giving praise
- reprimanding and giving constructive criticism

- giving bad news to someone
- handling people who delay your work
- negotiating
- resolving a difference of opinion
- persuading someone to use your services
- leading a productive meeting.

Appraisals – Giving feedback on performance

A key activity in performance management is the conversation between managers and their staff during which they discuss performance-enhancing ideas. While staff are often on the receiving end of performance feedback, it is rarely quality feedback. Consequently it is usually an uncomfortable experience for both manager and staff. Yet the power of quality feedback is so great that the appraisal process deserves significant attention from all managers.

Problems

Here are the main problems with the process of giving feedback:

- The purpose is rarely clear. Sometimes managers know the performance they want to be improved (and hence the behaviour they want the subordinate to change) but confuse the issue by talking about the subordinate's personality or attitude. The sudden bout of lateness is discussed as 'your deteriorating motivation'; the customer complaint is discussed as 'your poor attitude towards customers'.

- Open discussion can be hampered by the hierarchical relationship between managers and their staff. Managers see it as their role to 'take charge' of the discussion and subordinates feel threatened and defensive. Attempts to put subordinates at ease often backfire because they revolve around two minutes' idle chat about something irrelevant, such as the weather.
- Managers can feel uncomfortable giving feedback to staff where performance has been under par.
- Managers tend to talk too much and listen too little, with the result that subordinates rarely feel as if their views have been listened to sufficiently and they do not 'buy into' the same conclusions as the managers.

To overcome these problems and gain the benefits of giving feedback regularly to staff on their performance the following gameplan will help.

Prepare

- Prepare your staff and brief them clearly on the purpose of the discussion (namely, to improve working relationships and performance, not to tell them what the company thinks of them). Ensure they know they will be involved in the discussion as a participant, not as a recipient of information from you. Foster the thinking pattern that they are responsible for their performance, albeit with help from you.

- Prepare yourself. What were the key results or performance standards you agreed or expected? How has actual performance compared? What are the relevant behaviours you notice (as opposed to personality traits you assume)? Are your beliefs in order? You have a right to expect performance of a certain standard and to give feedback on performance. Your subordinate also has a right to be listened to, to be treated fairly, and to feel good about the discussion.
- Prepare the location. You need an environment where you will both be relaxed and feel all right about speaking frankly. That may require 'neutral' territory, such as a meeting-room.

Get the opening right

In just the same way that you have only one chance to make a first impression, the opening is your major sign-posting/focusing opportunity, so do not waste it. Impressions created in the first few seconds of the discussion will set up your subordinate's thinking patterns for the rest of it.

Conversations about the weather, traffic conditions, and families are productive only if relevant. Better to explain the purpose of the discussion and how you would like to go about it and ask if they feel OK about that. (This also serves to involve them within the first 15 seconds, which is what you should aim to do.)

Get the style right

Try adopting the following sequence for every 'section' of the discussion:

- Signpost – ie what you want to talk about and why.
- Use a question to encourage the subordinate to begin thinking and talking; continue that process by probing.
- Use your body language and tone of voice to stay neutral and relaxed, but attentive. Above all, avoid sounding like an interrogator or someone whose mind is already made up.
- Check your understanding of what they are saying, especially about concerns they have.
- Summarise what you have covered/agreed, etc.

Generally, a good discussion of this sort is characterised by the boss listening at least twice as much as he or she speaks, and probably more. You will therefore need to display a lot of listening behaviours to encourage your subordinate to talk. You will need to remember that probing, reflecting, and summarising are essential parts of active listening. The aim, remember, is to improve the subordinate's performance, so it helps if most of the ideas come from them. So you will need to use questions to encourage them to rethink their views.

If the appraisal is a productive one it is likely that you will need to speak frankly. To avoid the danger of triggering off an inappropriate reaction in the subordinate, pay special attention to avoiding emotive terminology and to maintaining a neutral tone of voice – but maintain the impact of what you are saying with direct eye contact.

Close effectively

Conclude the discussion with a summary of specific action. Merely agreeing to 'do something about . . .', or 'try to do better', or go on such and such a course 'some time soon' is the road to mediocrity. Be specific. Say, for example: 'So, I'm going to attend three sales meetings with you over the next two weeks from the list you supply tomorrow. I'll observe how you handle negotiations, without intervening, and then we'll be able to see how we can get these margins back up to target. Is that your understanding?'

A nice, and time-saving, touch if the discussion has been a long one is to ask your member of staff to produce a written summary within 24 hours. Handwritten will usually suffice. It has the effect of reassuring them that theirs is the version to be recorded.

Summary

1	*Prepare*	Look at the work tasks, objectives, problems, etc.
		Keep records; do not rely on memory.
		Encourage staff member to prepare.
2	*Get the opening right*	Minimal small talk.
		Outline the format of the discussion.
		Involve staff member within first few seconds.

Use body language to set tone of
discussion.

3 *Get the style
right*

Focus on behaviour, not personality or
attitude.

Be direct, accurate and concise; avoid
emotive language; be assertive.

Probe and reflect to encourage staff
member to think.

Listen at least 60 per cent of the time.

4 *Close effectively*

What will the staff member do to
improve performance? Agree specifics.
Summarise.

Giving praise

Encouraging and reinforcing the behaviour you want produces better and more predictable results than discouraging the behaviour you don't want. Consider this; there are two ways of house-training a puppy. One way is to wait until it puddles on the carpet, dip its nose in the mess and kick it out into the garden. As any psychologist will tell you, that is a very effective way of training the puppy to puddle on the carpet and run to the back door frightened. A more effective method of training is to take the puppy into the garden at regular intervals and, when it puddles where you want it to puddle, make a fuss of it. It works with people too; using praise to reinforce the behaviour you want increases the chances that you'll get it. So effective praising, while insufficient on its own, is an essential element in the way you influence others.

Problems

- Praising does not come naturally to most people, probably because our attention is drawn more readily to deviations than to norms, and the deviations we are primed to seek out are those that will cause us problems. In other words we find it easier to catch people doing something wrong than doing something right!
- When we do catch people doing something right, we are prone to contaminate the praise we give them, for example, by congratulating them on something while we search in the drawer for a missing file, turning the praise into a criticism: 'That was good. What a pity you can't do that more often.'

To overcome these problems and gain the benefits of praising staff, the following gameplan will help.

Praise quickly

The old saying 'strike while the iron is hot' is very apt. In praising, you are attempting to shape someone's behaviour and the praising will have most effect close to the actual event concerned. So praise as soon as possible after the event or, at least, as soon as you hear about it.

Be specific

You are praising because you want the other person to do more of the same, as it were, so you need to be sure they understand what 'more of the same' actually is. You need to be precise, therefore, in your terminology. 'That was good' is unlikely to be accurate enough whereas the following comment is much more precise: 'The way you stayed calm while that customer was ranting and raving was really impressive – and then you used that questioning technique to calm him down and get to the bottom of his complaint. That was good.'

Give it impact

You want the other person to feel good about the experience of being praised; you want to trigger their positive emotions. So:

- After describing the behaviour you are praising, state how you feel about it. This bit adds to the sincerity.
- Pause for a few seconds to let your remarks sink in.
- Maintain eye contact throughout.
- Smile, look pleased, look relaxed.

Milk it, but don't overegg it!

The results of effective praising can be so positive that it is worth squeezing the maximum benefit from it. There are two positive ways in which you can 'milk' a praising. First, probe. Ask the other person some questions about what they accomplished and how they went about it. 'What went through your mind when the customer came in?'; 'How did you manage to stay so calm?'; or 'How long did it take you to learn that?' Your purpose is to demonstrate interest, so the questions need to be genuine and the topic needs to be overtly worth the effort. Done correctly, this is a good positive and unconditional pat on the back.

Second, if the behaviour you are praising is significant enough, discuss what the other person learnt and see how that learning can be transferred to other aspects of their job. Say, for example, 'The questioning technique you used to help calm down that customer really worked well. How can you use that approach when Big John in dispatch loses his temper?' In this way your praising becomes a mini-coaching session.

There is a note of caution to sound, however. Praising can shape people's behaviour most effectively when it is intermittent. Praise too frequently, or praise trivial events, and you will devalue both the effect and your own credibility.

Close neatly

Again, with eye contact and a smile, encourage your subordinates to deliver more of the same. As good performance is something we all want from our staff and colleagues, it makes sense to use our behaviour to link our intentions to the results we want.

Praise makes us feel more secure and more valued. It makes us feel better about ourselves and it strengthens relationships. We like these feelings and so we do more of what earns the praise, even if the praise happens only intermittently.

Let's say that your boss rarely discusses priorities and one day you persevere and get him or her to suggest priorities. You could say, 'Thanks, it helps to know what needs to be done first. I feel more confident. I appreciate it when you spend a minute explaining priorities like that. Thank you.' And you accompany these words with the right eye contact, the right tone of voice, the right facial expression and, of course, the little pause for impact. You will stand a good chance of getting the priorities explained without asking next time.

Praising works in incremental steps. You are encouraging someone to move in the direction you want, so you do not have to wait until they are performing perfectly before you praise them.

Summary

1	*Praise quickly*	The closer to the event, the greater the impact of praising will be.
2	*Be specific*	Be precise and descriptive.
3	*Give it impact*	Provide impact by: – probing – state how you feel with a pause, eye contact, and a smile. See what aspects of behaviour can transfer to other tasks.
4	*Milk it, but don't overegg it*	Do not overdo it. Probe, to show interest. Draw out lessons for the future from present success.

5 *Close neatly*   Repeat the aspect you are praising.
Smile, with eye contact.
Thank the other person.

Reprimanding and giving constructive criticism

Giving praise is a powerful influencing tool because it 'shapes' behaviour. Occasionally, however, you have to let someone know that their behaviour is inappropriate or unacceptable. Again, there are effective and ineffective ways to do this.

Problems

- Few people enjoy reprimands or criticism. It hits the 'playback button' on negative experiences and unpleasant feelings emerge. This makes us less susceptible to change our behaviour positively.
- We can 'psych ourselves up' and go in too hard. This is usually characterised by exaggeration. 'You've been late twice this week' becomes 'I'm fed up with the way you're always coming in late these days.' A '10 per cent shortfall' becomes 'a wholly disgraceful performance'. It is as if we boost our case, and hence our confidence, by this exaggeration and generalisation. Alternatively, we can minimise the problem, in order to lessen the likelihood of confrontation. 'You've been late twice this week' becomes 'I hope you don't mind my

mentioning it, but...er...your timekeeping isn't
...er...quite as good as it...um...used to be.'
The '10 per cent shortfall' becomes 'just a teeny
little bit off-target'.

It will help, therefore, if you follow this gameplan.

Reprimand or criticise quickly

As with praising, the further away from the event, the
smaller will be the impact of a reprimand or criticism. So
act as soon as possible after the event, or as soon as you
hear about it – with two important provisos! If the event,
whatever it is, has caused your emotions to run very high,
consider delaying the reprimand or criticism until you
have calmed down. That way, you will be more rational
and less prone to exaggerate, use emotive language, make
assumptions, and so on. Also, avoid criticising in front of
other people.

Be specific

You are reprimanding or criticising because you want the
other person to do less of something, so you need to be
sure that they understand what that 'something' actually
is. So be precise in your terminology. As with praising, it
will help if you are clear in your own mind about exactly
what behaviour you want to discourage in others. Is it
laziness, lack of effort or commitment, slow responsive-
ness, not supporting the team, sloppy appearance, untidi-
ness, not sharing information, playing safe all the time, or
what?

One way you can be specific, ensure that you focus on

behaviour, and keep your own emotions in check, is to use the assertiveness technique of pointing out a discrepancy. Returning to the timekeeping example above, you might say, 'You've always been a good timekeeper but you've been late twice this week. Why is that?' Pointing out a discrepancy works equally well in more serious situations, for example: 'To complete this project on time I have had to enlist the resources of a variety of departments. Every departmental head has helped, even at great personal inconvenience, except for you. Why is that?'

This has the effect of being descriptive and non-judgemental; it also immediately involves the other person, making them less emotionally defensive. They still defend themselves but they will do so more openly and rationally.

Check you've got it right

Even if you are 100 per cent certain of your facts, still check that you have got it right. The reason for checking is twofold. First, there may just be a slight chance that you have not got the full picture. If the other person has genuine information that alters the situation then thank them for it and stop there. Do not press on through fear of losing face. You will lose infinitely more face by carrying on. Second, checking that you have got it right shows that, by allowing the other person to present their side, you are not jumping to conclusions. This adds to your credibility and the impact of the discussion. When the other person is responding, you need to show that you are listening with eye contact, head nods, reflecting, and summaries to check understanding.

When a reprimand is official, especially in uniformed occupations, you may find it appropriate to add to the formality of the occasion. The easiest way is to adopt a formal seating-arrangement, with the participants sitting opposite each other across a table or desk, and to sit formally (like a newsreader, upright, slightly forward, with hands clasped on the table in front of you). Please remember that the more formal the situation, the more your organisation's procedures will become relevant. The other person may have the right to a certain amount of notice of the discussion, to be accompanied by a colleague or union representative, and to recourse to a higher authority if they disagree with you. You will probably also have to produce a written record of the discussion. The aim, I would suggest, is to use reprimanding and criticising as positively as possible so that the formal situations become an infrequent last resort.

Give it some positive impact

To be effective, the reprimand or criticism must have positive rather than negative impact. You need to be concise without being blunt. The more you ramble, the less accurate you are. Pointing out a discrepancy helps here too. Stating how the event has made you feel (again accurately, without exaggeration), adds to the impact.

Your posture needs to be upright, open, and relaxed. If you feel anxious about the encounter, you may well 'close up' by crossing your legs tightly, 'shrinking' a little, protecting your abdomen, averting your eyes, and covering your mouth with your hand. If you feel angry about the event, this will show itself in a 'full-frontal' posture (head, torso and feet all facing the other person), an expansive chest, attacking gestures such as finger-wagging or finger-jabbing, and a tight-lipped facial expression with lowered eyebrows and excessive eye contact. Your tone of voice needs to be neutral rather than shaky or stern, your eye contact direct and relatively constant, but without the lowered eyebrows and tight lips of the angry person.

You might have to persist, rather than be fobbed off, by using the 'broken record' to make your point. You will have to let the other person know what the consequences will be if they do not change their behaviour as you have described. Here, you will need to pay special attention to your tone of voice. You want what you are saying to be received as a straightforward statement of cause and effect, not as a threat.

End on a high note

Remember, the other person must be left in no doubt what you want them to do differently, so repeat it. Also, you want them to remember the message, not the packaging, so remind them that your concern is with what has happened, not with them as a person. This applies whether the person you are criticising is a member of your staff, someone else's staff, a colleague, your child, your spouse, or your next-door neighbour. You are speaking up for what you want and trying to get the other person to agree with you. The more positively you handle the discussion, the better they will feel about it and the better your chance of success. To do that, your focus needs to be on the behaviour, your attention on the person, and your effort on the relationship.

Summary

1 *Reprimand or criticise*   Unless emotions are running very high.

2 *Be specific*   Be accurate:
  - no exaggeration
  - no minimalisation
  - no assumptions about personality or motives.

  No emotive language; point out a discrepancy.

  Pay attention to your eye contact, posture and tone of voice.

3 *Check you've got it right*   Listen.

4 *Give it some positive impact*   Pause, with eye contact.

  If necessary, use the 'broken record' and point out the consequence of not changing.

5 *End on a high note*   Focus on behaviour.

  Sound and look positive.

Giving bad news to someone

Of all the tasks we face, giving bad news to someone must be one of the most daunting.

Problems

- Knowing far in advance we have to pass on bad news sends our minds into overdrive about how awful it is going to be. Such self-talk is usually prone to exaggeration persuading us that the situation will be worse than it really is. The self-fulfilling prophecy ensures, however, that it is at least that bad!

- This negative self-talk makes us sugar-coat the message so that we feel better. One way of doing this is to beat about the bush, dragging out the actual announcement of the bad news and postponing the potential discomfort. This often unnerves the other person more than a blunt message.

- Sometimes we just do not stop talking. We deliver the message, explain the reason for it, explain that we know how the other person is feeling and describe what they need to do now, all without any involvement from the other person. It is almost as if we are afraid that the moment we stop talking they will start, and that is when the confrontation will begin. So if we talk continuously the problem will be deferred. We put off what we fear most, rush the other person, and make an unhappy situation worse.

- We seek comfort behind phrases that hide our real meaning. One of the all-time greats has to be, 'We're going to have to let you go,' as if the poor employee to whom we are talking has been straining at the leash for years waiting for the first opportunity to get free. What we really mean is, 'You're fired and I know you feel pretty sick about it; I just don't have the guts to come right out and say it.' More 'up-beat' varieties include '... affected by the recent skill-mix adjustments' and '... at variance with our future competency requirements'. The result is confusion and resentment.

In any situation where bad news is being delivered the outcome will never be pleasant. Rather than make matters worse we should, however, aim to minimise the other person's discomfort and, in so doing, minimise our own. A good measure of how effectively you deliver bad news is when the other person thanks you for the way you handled the announcement. Here is the gameplan.

Prepare

Depending on the severity of the bad news, the other person may be in a state of shock when you tell them. So, before you begin, put a support plan in place. In the case of redundancy, for example, it will be little use sending them back to their desks and expecting them to carry on as if nothing had happened. After you have made the announcement will someone be available to give them help and advice? Who will look after their work for the rest of the day or week? Put these plans in place before the discussion is held.

Signpost

If you act at all unusually the other person will pick up from your body language that something is amiss. Their thoughts will start racing as to what it could be, so it is far better to focus those thoughts at the beginning. Say, for example, 'Sandra, I need to talk to you for a moment. It's something important. Would you come in, please?' Your tone of voice and facial expression will indicate that it is something serious.

Give the reason, then the outcome

As you know, the company has been looking at staffing levels in relation to business forecasts and decided that a 10 per cent reduction in head-count is needed. Unfortunately, not enough volunteers have come forward and so there will be some compulsory redundancies. Everyone within five years of retirement age is to retire early. You come into that category, Sandra, so I am sorry to have to tell you that, from the end of next month, your job will be redundant.

If you give the news first and then the reason behind it, the reason is lost. It is like signposting a disagreement; no one listens to the reasons why. You may also find that, because we think much faster than someone talks, when presenting the information this way, they will get to the outcome slightly ahead of you.

Notice, please, that giving the reason first, then the outcome, need not take a long time. The example above takes about 12 seconds to say. Compare that with the way some people ramble on for a minute or so, deferring the actual announcement.

Listen

Having heard the bad news the other person's first reaction may be one of shock. Their thoughts are racing. They do not know what to say so they do not say anything. Neither should you. Give them time. Eventually they will speak and you will need to listen, but probably more passively than actively. Depending on the news they may be angry, sad, or any of a number of other feelings. They may give vent to their feelings by verbally attacking you. Remember that their emotions are running high and they may not speak kindly. So stay in control of your own emotions and do not take personally what they are saying.

Maintain the focus

Again, depending on the type of bad news, they may try to debate the issue. Stay focused, using the 'broken record' if necessary, and encourage them to stay focused too. 'Yes, you have been here a long time but the decision has been taken and your job is to be made redundant'; 'Yes, I know it feels unfair but the decision has been taken. It affects everyone in your age group.'

Use gentle probing to encourage them to focus their thoughts on future needs rather than on what have, abruptly, become past ones. If there is any assistance you can give (such as in this case redundancy counselling or pre-retirement planning) describing it now will help with the future focus.

Put the support plan into action

Put into action the support plan and keep informed of how it is progressing.

Summary

1 *Prepare*   Put together a support plan.

2 *Signpost*   Signpost that it will be an out-of-the-ordinary discussion; serious body language.
Be brief.

3 *Give the reason,* Be concise.
  then the   Neutral tone of voice and posture;
  outcome   keep eye contact.
Watch their body language.

4 *Listen*   Listen more passively than actively.
Stay in control of your emotions, no matter what the 'packaging'.

5 *Maintain the* Acknowledge what they are saying.
  focus   Use 'the broken record' to stay focused.
Gentle probing.

6 *Put the*   Action the plan and monitor its
  support plan progress.
  into action

Handling people who delay your work

One of the features of organisational life is that there are times when we depend on other people and they let us down. Here are the problems we encounter in such situations:

Problems

- Our frequent reminders have no effect. The people who have let us down seem immune to them.
- We approach them in a sympathetic way hoping for the co-operation we need. The result is that we feel bad for being so wimpish and they still fail to give us what we want.
- We send a last-ditch e-mail with veiled threats of what will happen if their co-operation 'is not forthcoming'. It does not come forth and we don't carry out our threats because we know it means losing face.
- Eventually, although we need their co-operation, they have so annoyed us that we go in with both guns blazing. The result is that we feel good temporarily but still fail to get what we want.

Here is a suggested gameplan. It may not work every time but it will work enough of the time to be of value.

Write it down

See the person who is letting you down face to face and, when you have agreed what assistance they are going to provide, write it down and let them see you writing it down. If the conversation is taking place over the telephone, ask them to hold while you write it down. Written commitments are always stronger than oral ones.

Appeal to their integrity

Ask them straight: 'Can I count on you for that?' Look them directly in the eye and nod as you ask the question. As we tend to mirror another person's body language, they will probably nod as they confirm that you can indeed count on them. Very few people will respond, 'Actually, I'm a lying toad.'

Use subtle 'bribery'

There is a saying in negotiating that goes, 'trade, don't concede'. That is why you will hear negotiators say things like 'If you [do this], I'll [do that]' and 'I can only agree [to this] if you can agree [to that].' You can use this principle to 'bribe' the other person: 'If you bring me that information on the 17th, I'll buy you a [beer, coffee, or whatever it is worth].' (Notice the confirmation of the date by which you agreed the information would be supplied.) You can add to this bribery by a subtle little change: instead of 'If you bring me...' you can say, *'When* you bring me...'. This creates a more positive and permanent vision in the other person's mind.

Explain the benefits

Most of us do things because we perceive a personal benefit in it. It might be that we feel good when we help someone, or that we know we would feel guilty if we did not. You will know the person from whom you want this information and also whether they need more tangible benefits. If the information they are providing is substantial maybe they deserve a bigger reward than a cup of coffee or a glass of beer. So, if appropriate, you can finish off the 'bribery' sentence with '...and I'll tell your boss how helpful you've been'. This also carries the implication that if they do not deliver the information by the agreed date you will pass on that news instead.

Thank them

If the event has been significant enough, a short praising might be appropriate here. (You feel good when you know you can rely on them, you know this report will be a good team effort, you know the customer will appreciate the amount of work that has gone into it, etc.) At the very least they deserve a genuine thankyou. That means one given with a smile, eye contact, and an attentive posture (not delivered over your shoulder on the way out of their office).

Summary

1	*Write it down*	This adds to their commitment.
2	*Appeal to their integrity*	Make eye contact; nod so that they 'mirror'.
3	*Use subtle 'bribery'*	'When you . . . , I'll . . .'
4	*Explain the benefits*	Be very concise.
5	*Thank them*	Make eye contact; smile. Pause.

This approach may look contrived. It is, however, preferable to being aggressive, submissive, moaning, or complaining to their boss, etc. Try to use it naturally and it will have positive effects.

Negotiating

Negotiating is on the increase. Budgets are becoming tighter so managers are pushing for bigger discounts and fighting for resources, negotiating with colleagues over resources, staff, time-scales, availability, and so on. Domestically, increases in joint breadwinner households, homeworking and parental pressures mean we are negotiating more with family members.

Problems

- Mind-set. This is the big one, from which all the other problems stem. People see the process as a kind of tug-of-war where what one party gains the other, by definition, has to lose. This encourages them to try several different tactics. They may try to attempt to manipulate or trick the other party. When dealing with a salesperson, for example, they may keep him or her waiting, suddenly but deliberately cut short the meeting on a pretext, leave a competitor's brochure just visible in a strategic position and demand 'your best price!' When dealing with someone internally they may try to pull rank, to flatter, or to present a logical argument to convince the other person that their cause is more essential to organisational success than the other person's. They may try to gain concessions with tricks, threats, and posturing. Pretending to withdraw from the negotiations if their 'very reasonable' demands are not met is a favourite. Telling lies is another.

- People making goodwill concessions on the assumption they will be reciprocated. Usually the reverse happens: it convinces the other person that if they sit tight, more concessions will follow.

What we need is therefore a gameplan that facilitates co-operation without leaving us exposed or committed to unilateral concessions.

Question in order to broaden

There are four potential outcomes to any negotiation: win/lose, lose/win, lose/lose and win/win. Unless you are dealing with the release of hostages or some such other extreme situation there is only one outcome worth considering – win/win. Fundamental to negotiating is the principle of trading rather than conceding.

By trading creatively you can handle negotiations to achieve a win/win outcome, even when the other party is thinking solely of win/lose. Before you can begin to trade, however, you need to broaden the issue under discussion, and to do that you need to probe to find out what is important to the other person. This will enable you to identify the other person's perception of value. If you have something they value then you have good bargaining power, especially if that something will cost you little.

For example, if a speedy delivery is critical to the other person and your delivery van will be in their area tomorrow, your bargaining power has just gone up. If they want your subject-matter expert next week, and the project on which she is currently working is due to end this Friday, your bargaining power has just gone up. If the safety implications of a new directive are important to the other person, and you have the only safety expert in the company, your bargaining power has just gone up.

But you will discover these things only if you question on a broad front. To broaden the discussion you may need to signpost well. Try questions such as 'I'd like to make sure I understand the background to this discussion. May I ask you a few general questions, please?' This may do the trick.

Link in order to trade

Often, to give yourself more bargaining power you need to be creative about what you link together when you start trading. By way of illustration, the usual items that salespeople link are price and volume: 'I can increase the discount only if you increase the quantity you order.' They could also add in other aspects of the deal such as time-scales to delivery, storage of the goods, warranties, after-sales service, returns policies, money-back guarantees, and even add in aspects of the relationship such as technical advice, staff training, marketing endorsements, referrals, first opportunity to tender for the next deal, etc. All it takes is a little lateral thinking, which is easily stimulated by the amount of questioning you do.

Stick to the core skills

You need to probe and listen. All the productive questions have a role in the negotiating, and you need to listen actively. Open questions, reflecting, and pausing will encourage the other person to talk. Hypothetical questions will help test the water and are especially useful when you start trading. Closed questions are useful for checking. Summarising and checking your understanding, especially when used with signposting and self-disclosure, will not only help you stay on the same wavelength; they will help you be seen as open and honest.

Work on rapport. Avoid being dogmatic, disagreeing, and using 'irritators', and use the more productive triggers such as seeking ideas, making suggestions, building, and supporting.

Control of your own body language and awareness of the other person's are vital. You want to give away little with your own body language while ensuring that it supports the words you are speaking. I once observed a negotiating role-play between a young female scientist and an estate agent. He was winning easily, yet she was doing everything according to the book – except for one thing.

I stopped the role-play after about 10 minutes and privately pointed out to her that every time she wanted to make a serious point she averted her gaze to the table. I asked her to make deliberate eye contact with every serious sentence. The role-play resumed and the estate agent capitulated after two minutes. His comment, when I asked him why he gave up so soon, was interesting. He said, 'This time she means it.' Even more interesting was that he could not tell me how he knew – he just knew! Your eye contact, tone of voice, posture, and gestures all need to be positive.

As you observe the other person's body language watch for clusters of disapproval (leaning back, arms folded, head tilted back slightly), lying (eye shiftiness, hand to nose), impatience (tight lips, loud exhalation, faster breathing), consideration (chin-stroking, upward gaze), and so on.

Remember the key lessons of assertiveness. As well as controlling tone of voice and eye contact, be concise rather than rambling, be prepared to say what you want, and use the 'broken record' to stand your ground while encouraging movement from the other person.

Summary

1 *Question in order to broaden*	Probe and listen. Round up as much information as possible. Look for benefits to the other person that cost you little. Weigh up your bargaining power.
2 *Link in order to trade*	Be creative; think relationship as well as product or service.

3 *Stick to the core skills*	Ask for ideas about what they want.
	Build on those ideas.
	Suggest rather than propose.
	Use 'If I . . . , will you . . . ?' questions.
	Maintain a relaxed posture; eye contact is especially important for serious remarks.
	Use the 'broken record' to encourage movement on the other person's part.

Negotiating is not a tug-of-war. When it does become one, relationships and effectiveness deteriorate. It is instead about trading and creativity. When these two characteristics are evident it is often possible to arrive at a better joint solution than either party could have dreamed up independently.

Resolving a difference of opinion

This section has many similarities to that on negotiating, so if you have not already done so, you might like to read the preceding section.

Problems

- Some people have a win/lose mind-set. They are incredibly competitive and adopt an adversarial approach even though they and the other person may be 'on the same side'. Aiming to win at the expense of the other person makes little sense. Whether they are a colleague, a customer, or a supplier, they are all part of the same extended team. Where significant principles are at stake a steadfast approach may be admirable, but if overused it is called 'stubborn'.

- Some people have a consensus mind-set and try not to rock the boat. They see conflict as something to be avoided rather than as an energy which, if harnessed, can produce positive results. While the consensus approach may be relevant to some issues, it can produce the proverbial camel when what we want is a racehorse. Reducing issues to the lowest common denominator is the road to mediocrity.

What we need is a mind-set that enables us to see what sort of differences we are dealing with, so that we can react accordingly.

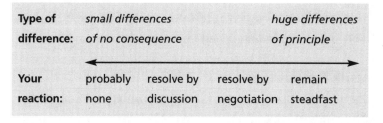

Type of difference:	small differences of no consequence			huge differences of principle
Your reaction:	probably none	resolve by discussion	resolve by negotiation	remain steadfast

For small differences, all you might need to do is listen so as better to understand people. For bigger differences you may need to engage in discussion, listening to their viewpoint and explaining your own. As you move up the scale you may need to start trading and, finally, there may be some issues where you have to remain intransigent, explaining your viewpoint carefully. Each of these stages could be a separate discussion or represent different elements in the same discussion.

The trick to resolving a difference of opinion is first seeking to understand and then seeking to be understood. So the gameplan is based on the persuasive funnel.

Probe and listen

Listen to the other person's proposal, probe to find out what they want from it, how they see their proposal delivering what they want, and on what beliefs they are working. Use open questions to gain information and closed questions to check your understanding. Control your body language so you come across as someone who is seeking to understand rather than interrogate, or as someone who is signalling disagreement. Signposting will help.

The very least that will happen is that if you do need to dig in and fundamentally disagree you will appear more reasonable than you would otherwise have done, because you will have listened and considered.

Look for overlap

Look for areas where your interests coincide. Use building and suggesting to establish in the other person's mind the cause and effect between what they want and what you want (which might now be different from your reaction when you first heard what they wanted). Remember to express your suggestion in terms they will find attractive, that is, in terms of the benefits to *them* rather than in terms of the benefits to *you*, or in terms of the features of your suggestion.

Praise them

When you reach an agreement, praise the other person in some way. They have listened and discussed and reconsidered their proposal. You want to encourage this behaviour so praise them for listening, for putting the company first, acting in the customers' interests, or whatever. That way, next time they may bounce their ideas off you first, thus giving you a better chance of altering their views while they are still fresh and before they begin to set hard.

Summary

1 *Probe and listen* Round up information.
Probe to understand both details and beliefs.
Search for benefits the other person hopes their proposal will bring.
Check your understanding.

2 *Look for overlap* Build on what the other person says they want.
Express your suggestions in terms of benefits to them.
Be prepared to trade.
Maintain a relaxed posture; eye contact is especially important for serious remarks.
Use the 'broken record' to encourage movement on their part.

3 *Praise them* Thank them for working with you to produce a solution from which

company, customers or whoever will benefit.

Persuading someone to use your services

Whether you are in sales, are self-employed, have to charge other departments for your services or have to present recommendations to senior management, this game-plan is for you.

Problems

- The main fault here, from which all the others stem, is the assumption that, just because we can see the logic of our case, the other person will too.
- We forget that people buy something to fulfil a need. Whether they are spending their own money or their department's budget, if they fail to see the need or fail to see that what you have to offer will satisfy their need, they will not be persuaded.
- We present our case from our viewpoint and in our terms. We describe what makes sense to us and what is attractive to us on the misguided assumption that it will also make sense to the other person, and that they will find the same things attractive. We describe the features of the product or service and not the benefits those features will deliver to the other person. We use our jargon rather than theirs. As a result we

widen the communication gap rather than close it.

- We talk too much and listen too little. We believe that giving information is an effective way of influencing – whereas, by asking the right questions and listening to the answers, we can find out exactly how to present our case.

- We fail to spot the little signals indicating that the other person is interested. Questions such as 'Is it available in red?', 'How soon could you deliver?', 'If I agreed, how long would implementation take?' are the signs of interest.

- We are 'thrown' by objections. As soon as the other person disagrees with something that we say, or presents an obstacle to agreeing with us, we have difficulty handling it.

Effective influencers recognise these problems and overcome them by seeking to understand the other person's situation and problems, by involving the other person in the conversation and helping them appreciate fully how the product or service will benefit them. They do so by using the persuasive funnel.

Round-up (probe and listen)

Effective influencers first 'round up' information about the other person's situation, priorities and constraints. This is an information-gathering phase and may well need signposting as such to ensure that you and the other person are on the same wavelength. You could ask, 'Before I explain my proposal to you, may I put to you a few questions to ensure that I understand your situation?'

If the other person is pressed for time or is in a rush to 'get down to business' you might have to persevere with the 'broken record'.

> *Don't bother with the questions. Just tell me what you've got to say.*
> I'm happy to explain it to you, I just want to do so in terms that are relevant, so I'd still like to ask you a few questions, please.
> *I'll be the judge of whether it's relevant.*
> I know you will. However, there is usually more than one way of explaining something and I think it's in your interest that I explain it the right way for you and your situation, so I'd like to ask you a few questions, please.

The questions you ask will depend on what you are 'selling' and how much you already know. If the situation is brand-new to you, you may need to start very broadly with structure, business processes, objectives, plans, and constraints. If you are already familiar with the situation, you may just need to concentrate on the issue you are there to discuss. Either way you will want plenty of open questions, reflecting, checking that you understand, and summarising.

It is worth pointing out that customers often find that the process of you seeking information not only helps to clarify the situation in their minds but also helps them see proof that you are genuine in your recommendations.

Reason (focus, reflect, summarise)

Your round-up of information should, with luck, high-light areas that will prove fruitful for further probing. In the section on probing and listening we looked at the example of a computer salesman who discovered that his potential customer's current computer was slow, unreliable, and required too much manual intervention. The salesman then probed even further to determine the full implications of the problem which, in this case, were difficult month-ends, expensive contract staff, and dissatisfied customers: potential reasons for buying a new computer, which the salesman mentally noted.

It is during this stage that summarising is particularly fruitful because you can use it to focus the other person's attention on the problem and its implications.

Result (relate to situation, suggest)

'Result' refers to the benefits the customer will gain by buying your product or service. Or the benefit the other person will gain by agreeing to your proposal. There are two points to keep in mind during this stage. The first is to remember that a single compelling reason for doing something is a more powerful persuader than a whole stack of reasons. A whole stack of reasons can make you sound desperate and, because they are unlikely to be all as strong as one another, the other person can easily attack the weakest. So stick to a single compelling reason. You can always hold the others in reserve, should you need them.

The second point is that you want the other person to visualise the benefits they will gain. Visualisation can be a very powerful persuader – that is why so many advertisements on television and in magazines display a lifestyle, not just a product. The implication is that by chewing this gum you will become more carefree, by smoking these cigarettes you will gain greater enjoyment of the great outdoors, or by driving this motor car you will experience the charisma of a successful executive.

Questions can help the other person visualise. Returning to our computer salesman, he asks the customer, 'What would be the effect on your need for contract staff if you had a reliable computer?' He knows that the use of contract staff is a concern of the customer and that cost is another major concern. He knows these things because the customer told him in response to his questions. That is what the customer will 'buy', even though he will pay for a computer.

Knowing what will be attractive to the customer is easier if you watch for 'buying signals'. These are expressions of interest. They might be in the form of fairly obvious questions like those shown above, eg 'How long would implementation take?' That kind of question shows interest because few people would enquire about implementation time-scales if they had already decided against implementation. Some buying signals, however, are more subtle. If in response to one of your points the other person exhibits a cluster of behaviours indicating consideration (finger and thumb to chin, head slightly inclined to one side, with eyes looking upwards) it would be worth checking to see if you have just scored a point.

It is during this last stage that the other person may raise objections. Salespeople are often taught to overcome objections. This indicates a mind-set that sees objections as obstacles between you and 'sale'. Consequently, salespeople are taught techniques to overcome the obstacles. A price objection, for example, might be tackled with a 'reduce to the ridiculous' tactic. A computer costing several thousand pounds might be 'too expensive' but one that 'costs only £2 a day', based on a four-year life, may not be.

A more productive mind-set is to think of objections as stepping-stones. If you satisfy the other person on a particular point, you get that much closer to the decision. This attitude will encourage you to be more assertive. So if the other person says, 'I'd like to think about it' you might probe, 'What do you want to think about?' That way genuine objections are brought into the open and you can discuss them rationally. For example:

> *I'm not sure. I'd like to think about it.*
> That's fine. I'm glad you want to think about it. What exactly do you want to think about? We've established that your reduced use of contract staff will effectively pay for the computer so there will be no negative cash flow.
> *There's a lot of change in the company at the moment. I'm wondering if my staff can handle learning a new computer system.*
> Is that the only thing you want to think about?
> *Yes.*
> If I can satisfy your concern on this issue is there anything else on which you would need reassurance?

No, that would be it.

OK, may I explain how the two computers compare?

Please do.

Overcoming an objection with trickery is not the way to make a customer satisfied with the process or with the outcome. Engaging them in rational discussion is much more productive and it is more acceptable to people who want long-term relationships.

Summary

1	*Round-up*	An information-gathering phase. Signpost so the other person appreciates why you need to ask them so many questions. Use open questions and reflecting.
2	*Reason*	Continue probing to uncover the full extent of their problems and the issues they want to address. Listen intently: they may not even realise the significance of some of the things they say.
3	*Result*	Use hypothetical questions to help them see the full benefits that you are offering. Look for 'buying signals'. Probe objections.

Leading a productive meeting

Very few people enjoy meetings. The criticisms are consistent: they last too long, take up too much time and achieve too little; they could be better managed. In addition, meetings are a bit of a 'shop window', especially when they are attended by someone senior. Some people like to show off in them to get noticed. The best way to get noticed, however, is to manage the process of the meeting, or to contribute towards the management of the meeting, positively.

Problems

- There is insufficient notice and hence insufficient preparation time.
- The start is postponed to allow latecomers to arrive; the time of punctual people is thus wasted. This is a good way of ensuring that meetings start later and later as more and more people choose not to waste time waiting. So they arrive when they think the meeting will start.
- Discussions ramble and people lose sight of why an item is on the agenda.
- The minutes take too long to prepare and are at variance with people's memories.
- They are staggeringly expensive. If you were to add up the employment costs of everyone at your next meeting you would probably be in for a shock.

Here is a gameplan that will help eradicate these problems:

Before the meeting

Distribute a meeting plan in sufficient time before the meeting. The plan is a device to streamline the meeting. It should first state the purpose of the meeting. If it is not clear, cancel the meeting. Next, it should state who is attending and what contribution is expected from them. If they have no contribution, do they need to be there? If their attendance is due to their need to be informed why not let them have the minutes to read or an audiotape of the meeting which they can listen to at their convenience? Estimate the cost of the meeting by calculating approximate salaries plus on-costs (your personnel manager should be able to advise). Plus the expenses for the meeting. This tends to reduce the number of 'meeting groupies' who have no contribution but who feel obliged to say something once they are there. Finally, display an objective agenda. That is, for each item state why it is there – for example, 'To confirm marketing department's recommendation regarding...' or 'To choose one of the short-listed training providers' or 'To consider the issues involved in performance-related pay so that a circular can be produced for staff'. This helps you to stay on track.

During the meeting

First, unless there are specific and one-off reasons for not doing so, start on time. Do not wait for latecomers. Nor recapitulate for them. Take the important decisions first. This usually encourages punctuality.

Second, stay on track. Many of the skills we have covered will assist you – for example, signposting: 'Let's first of all look at all the good points in this proposal and then we'll look at the bad points.' Then probing when someone is straying: 'How does what you are saying relate to this item?' or 'How does what you are saying help us make this decision?' You are giving people a chance to justify themselves, which is fair. If they cannot, your question will have more effect than a blunt 'Shut up.' Summarising is a very productive way of pulling together various aspects of the discussion either to check your understanding or to make a decision. Remember, too, that behaviours can trigger fairly predictable responses, so suggest rather than propose, and seek clarification rather than disagree. If you have to disagree directly do not signpost it; explain your reason first, then disagree.

If you have a choice, arrange the seating so that you can see everyone's body language. That way you can tell who wants to say something but is afraid to speak, who is confused but reluctant to ask, and who disagrees but does not say so.

Third, listen actively not only so that you can understand but also so that you can help less gifted contributors make their point. Also, avoid leading questions such as 'Right, does anybody want to disagree with me on this one?' If you are the most senior person there, that approach can be tempting.

Fourth, remember your role as conductor of the orchestra. If people mix suggesting, building, factual probing, negative thinking, and describing their feelings, the meeting will get out of tune, as it were. As the conductor, you can engender harmony and progress by ensuring that everyone talks about only one aspect at a time. It might be worth rotating the chairperson role every meeting or appointing someone to act as process manager. Their role is to observe and comment on the process of the meeting but not to take part in it. Their input is to say things such as 'Jean made a relevant point there but it got lost in the general hubbub. It might be worth repeating' or 'You appear to be going around in circles on this one. Would you like me to summarise the opposing views so that you can make a decision?'

Finally, control time. Use the estimated cost figures to keep people on track – for example, remark that 'So far we've clocked up £200 discussing the relative merits of these two options. As the difference in cost between them is only £250 shall we make a decision?'

At the end of the meeting

Unless you need a verbatim record of the meeting for, say, legal reasons, keep the minutes to a minimum. Consider bullet-point minutes listing the decisions reached and who is responsible for what. Have them written as the meeting progresses, copied immediately the meeting ends, and distributed before people leave. Not only is it more efficient but it adds to the overall image of an efficiently run, no-nonsense meeting.

Summary

1 *Before the
  meeting*

Distribute a meeting plan that states
the meeting's purpose; those who are to
attend and their expected contribution;
the cost and objectives of each agenda
item.

2 *During the
  meeting*

Start on time.
Take the important decisions first.
Use full range of core skills depending
on agenda items (eg persuading,
negotiating).
For process management, use signposting, probing, summarising, suggesting,
and seeking clarification.
Observe others' body language.
Consider appointing a process
manager.

3 *At the end of
  the meeting*

Brief bullet-point minutes of decisions
taken and who is responsible for what.
Distribute minutes at end of meeting.

8

Implementation

Let's begin this final chapter with a brief review. Here are the main points.

- Behaviour is the link between our intentions and the results we actually achieve. In order to achieve what we intend to achieve we need to be skilled in both what we do and in how we do it. Because much of what we achieve is with or through other people, interpersonal skills are essential.

- There are only a few interpersonal skills. In the same way as a cook will use the same basic ingredients to create a variety of dishes we can mix together our core skills in different ways depending on the situation we are in.

- Interpersonal skills can be used manipulatively or positively. Using them positively produces better results. Using them positively means recognising three principles that relate to influencing people – manipulative influencing has disadvantages for you, the penny has to drop in the other person's mind, and your behaviour is your influencing tool.

- A positive approach to influencing other people

is an essential life skill. To influence people effectively, you need *positive* influencing skills.

All you need to do now is *implement* what you have learned. Learning and then using new skills is a gratifying experience but it is a bit trickier than many people realise.

The tricky bit!

The problem is *habit*. When we are *learning* a new skill, we use the conscious part of our mind. We have to *think* about what we are doing. When we have *learned* it, we store it in the subconscious part of our mind. This means we can perform the new skill *without thinking* about it. It has become habit. Practising a new skill long enough for it to become habit can take weeks or even months.

The problem comes during the transitional stage when we have to think about the new skill while we practise it because the conscious part of our mind can think about only a limited number of things at once. So if it is needed to think about something complex, or if it is put under pressure, say by someone acting manipulatively towards us, there is insufficient thinking capacity left over to concentrate on the new skills. This is when our old habits take over and we 'revert to type'. What we need, therefore, are some suggestions to help us turn the new skills into habit quickly. Here are five ideas to help the habit-forming process.

Think of stepping-stones

Sometimes the size of a task can be very daunting. The gap between what we want to achieve and where we are now seems too huge to leap. My advice is: do not even try! Use stepping-stones instead.

Stepping-stones make large gaps easier to cross. All you have to do is take a problem one step at a time. Ask yourself, 'To remove this obstacle, what is the first thing I have to do, and the second, and the third, and so on?' For example, let us say that you want to stop Bill behaving in a certain way towards you and the change is a big one to achieve; the stepping-stones may look like this:

Step 1	Step 2	Step 3	Step 4	Step 5
Choose an appropriate time and place	Explain that I want to raise a sensitive issue	Describe what it is I prefer Bill not to do and explain why	Describe how I would like our relationship to be	Ask Bill how he feels about what I've just said

Whatever the obstacle or task, this technique helps break it down into manageable proportions and, even if you do not get all the way to the end, you might get farther along than you may have done in the past. That means you are progressing. You are gradually implementing what you have learned.

Have mental dress-rehearsals and mental replays

Our imagination can appear very real to us and, with a little practice, we can imagine anything we like. You can use this ability in two ways. The first is to have a *mental dress-rehearsal*. Think of a situation that is going to happen: imagine how you will open the conversation, how the other person will react, how good you will feel when you stay calm, and how you will use your core skills. This is as good as a real-life dress-rehearsal, if not better, because you can make the conversation go exactly the way you want, rewind and play certain bits again, fast forward, etc. So when the situation arises in reality, you have already experienced it and, effectively, *practised* how you will handle it. Athletes, sports people and musicians practise this way all the time.

The second way to use this interplay between imagination and reality is to replay events that have already taken place. Not all situations give you time to prepare. Neither do they all go according to plan. So, just like replaying a video, you have a *mental replay* of the event to look at how you performed, what you did that helped, what you did that hindered, and how you would handle the situation differently next time. Then you can imagine the situation going exactly as you would have hoped.

This is not idle fantasy. Top sports people have learned the importance of a positive image of themselves and their ability. Many golfers, for example, having hit a bad shot, will replay it in their minds, imagining it going as they had intended, before moving on to the next shot. This way, the image they retain in their minds is a positive one. If it helps them, it will help you too.

Keep a learning log

Experience can be a great teacher – but only if it is used properly. Far too often we forget to *reflect* on what happens to us and then we learn nothing from it. So, in addition to reviewing the key points of each chapter, you might like to keep a written record of your experiences as you implement what you have learned. You can describe the situation, what happened, what you learned and how you will use that learning in the future. By building up a series of learning logs, you can chart your progress.

Learn more

Further reading is an excellent way to maintain your interest in, and improve your knowledge of, a subject; here, then, is a selection of books that you may find useful.

GILLEN T. *Assertiveness for Managers*. Aldershot, Gower, 1992.
A thorough text explaining in detail what assertiveness is and how it applies to a variety of situations in which managers and other people find themselves. As one reviewer put it, 'You ought to read this. No – try again: there are messages here you cannot afford to miss.'

GILLEN T. *Assertiveness*. London, IPD, 1997.
A quick up-to-date guide on learning and using assertiveness.

HONEY P. *Problem People...And how to manage them*. London, IPD, 1992.
An A-Z guide to handling problem people.

LABORDE G. *Influencing with Integrity*. St Clears, Anglo-American Book Co, 1995.
A detailed look at the increasingly popular subject of neuro-linguistic programming (NLP for short).

FORSYTH P. *Making Meetings Work*. London, IPD, 1998.

FURNHAM A. *Body Language at Work*. London, IPD, 1999.

KNIGHT S. *Introducing NLP*. London, IPD, 1999.

MacKay I. *Listening Skills*. London, IPD, 1998.
Quick, easy-to-read guides in the Management Shapers series from the IPD.

Pease A. *Body Language*. London, Sheldon Press, 1981.
A well-presented, fully illustrated, and useful book on the subject.

Spread the word

What will you do with your positive influencing skills? Will you use them to get on better with that difficult neighbour; to ensure that the garage carries out the service properly this time; or to finish the next meeting of the Parent-Teacher Association in record time? With whom will you share the skills? – your colleagues, your children, your spouse or partner?

A final thought

This book has been designed to help you improve your powers of influence, but to do so positively rather than manipulatively. In that way, you not only achieve more of what you want, you build relationships based on openness, trust, understanding and mutual respect. The more people there are who influence positively, the more we shall listen to one another, try to understand one another and more easily make ourselves understood. We shall be more open and honest with one another. We shall be better to work with, to be with and to live with. I hope, therefore, that you will spread the word. That has to be good. It passes my TSR Test. I hope it passes yours.

Good luck!

Index

accuracy in expression 48–9
active listening *see* listening, active
aggressive behaviour 44, 45, 47, 48, 53, 62, 93, 127
appraisals 102, 103–108
appraisal skills xiv, 75–6, 78–9
asking the right questions 20–25, 26, 137
assertiveness, being assertive 40, 43–63, 83, 108, 131
  definition of 43–6, 53
  techniques of 47–52, 115
  see also thinking assertively

bad news, passing on 103, 118–123
  minimising discomfort for all concerned 119–120
behaviour as an influencing tool 2, 11–14, 47–52, 148
  as a whole repertoire or tool kit 12
  gearing it towards an objective 11, 46–7, 111, 148
body language 6, 46, 47, 55, 64–6, 73, 89–101, 106, 108, 121, 123, 125, 130–131, 134, 135, 145, 147
  behavioural clusters in 91–2, 95, 131, 140
  'buying signals' 140, 142

congruency in 92
cultural aspects of 93
gestures 98–100, 131
lying and 90, 131
matching as an indication of rapport 64–6, 125, 126
perceiving and understanding 90–101, 130, 145, 147
posture and 94–100
proximity 96–8
the importance of 89–90
the timing of changes in 91–2
books for further reading 152–3
bribery 2, 125–6
'broken record' (continued repetition), the *see* manipulation, avoidance of by the 'broken record'; repetition, the 'broken record'
building a rapport *see* rapport-building
'bulldozing' 53, 55, 77
bulls**t, avoiding 18
bullying 2, 4
business process re-engineering xii

chairperson, the position of 85–6, 146

checking information/one's
understanding *see*
information, checking
commitment once influenced
8–9
communication, the process of
28–30
the skills/competence
involved in xiii
see also transmission of
communication
comprehension of the
persuader's logic 1, 9–11,
14, 38, 148
conciseness, being concise 48,
123, 131
conflict situations 33–4, 44, 48,
94, 133
consequence, pointing out
51–2
controlling a conversation
16–17
conversationalist, becoming a
18–19
co-ordinating an approach for
group discussion *see*
group, co-ordinating a
discussion for a
core skills in influencing *see*
assertiveness, being
assertive; influencing
others positively, in
groups; persuasive
probing; rapport-building
counselling xv, 27, 122
the skills involved in xiv
counter-proposals as rapport-
breakers 77
credibility, improvement in
xiv, 34, 96, 115
reduction in 4, 111
criticism, constructive 102,
113–118

positive impact with
116–118
customer care considerations
xii
creativity xiii

defence/attack spirals 77–8
delay, people who cause 103,
123–7
de-layering, the effects of
xii
difference of opinion *see*
disagreement
disagreement 2, 13, 17, 103,
121, 132–6, 137, 145
being dogmatic as a trigger
of 77, 130
fear of 9
resolution of 103, 132–6
response to 13, 17
displacement activity 99

embarrassment 7
embedded suggestions *see*
suggesting, embedded
explaining one's own feelings
see feelings, explaining
one's own
eye contact 31, 45–6, 47, 61,
91, 93, 100, 107, 110, 111,
112, 113, 115, 117, 118,
123, 126, 130–131, 135

feedback on performance *see*
performance feedback
feelings, explaining one's own
32, 34, 49, 112, 116
fight-or-flight response, the
43–4, 48, 54
formality and formal
procedures 116
'formalspeak' 73–4
fundamental principles 1–15

gameplans, tactics or strategies for influencing 102–147
gestures *see* body language, gestures
group, co-ordinating a discussion for a 84–8
influencing 83–8
the discussion process in a 85–8
wavelength 83–6
guilt, feelings of 7, 9
as a manipulative tactic 61–2

habit-forming process, ways to speed the viii, 149–153
home working considerations xiii, 127
Honey, Peter 76

implementation of (new) interpersonal/influencing skills, the 148–153
influencing others positively viii, xi, xiii–xiv, 8–9, 38–40, 43, 102–147, 148–9
core skills for 15, 16, 102, 148, 151
definition of xiv
fundamental principles of 1–15
in groups 83–8
testing your current methods of 14–15, 100–101
the skills involved in xiv–xv, 1, 43, 149
information, checking 21, 22, 31, 115–116, 130, 134, 135, 138, 145
decoding *see* transmission of communication, integration and decoding of

obtaining 16, 20, 24, 25, 27–8, 33, 131, 134, 135, 137, 142
retrieval 30–32
storage 30–32
interpersonal skills/competence vii, ix, xii–xiv, 7, 16, 148–153
irritators 74–6
IT, the effects of introduction and use of xii

jargon 14, 30–31, 136

knowledgeable, appearing to be 18

learning, memorable experiences in 7
learning log 151–2
listening, active 12–13, 19, 22, 25, 27, 28–32, 33–4, 39, 46, 63, 67, 72–3, 88, 106, 108, 118, 122, 123, 130, 131, 134, 135, 137–8, 142, 145
lack of 3, 12, 17, 22, 31–2, 104
'on the same wavelength' 68–70, 137
passive 28, 30–32, 122, 123, 133
'logic' that is spurious/warped 2–8, 12, 55–7

managerial skills, current 43
old-style viii, xii
manipulation by others of oneself 43, 53–63, 73, 148
avoidance of by the 'broken record' 50–51, 55
forms and techniques of 53–63

manipulation of others by
oneself, intended 2–4, 8,
47, 127, 148
lack of any 38
reasons behind 6–8
unintended 4–6, 8, 40
manipulative influencing, the
disadvantages of 1, 2–9, 148
matrix teams xii
meeting, the productive 103,
143–7
controlling (the process of)
the 144–6
mental dress-rehearsals/mental
replays 150–151
motivation of others 8, 79
as compared with
manipulation 8, 9

negative emotions/memories
8, 113
the impact of 7
negotiating 103, 125, 127–132,
133, 147
negotiating skills xiv, 43, 125
trading rather than making
concessions 125, 128,
129–130, 132, 133
neuro-linguistic programming
(NLP) 78

objections, handling 141–2
obstacles to interpersonal skills
improvement viii
outsourcing viii
'ownership' (wholehearted
commitment) 8–9
lack of 2

pacing one's thinking 66–8, 70,
73
parental-style language as
rapport-breaker 74

passive listening see listening,
passive
patronising behaviour 40, 45,
53
'penny dropping in someone's
mind' see comprehension
of the persuader's logic
performance feedback 102,
103–8
effective closing 107, 108
opening 105, 107
problems with 103–4
style of presentation 106–7,
108
persistence, being persistent
43, 45, 117, 138
personal defence shield 62–3
personal tool kit 12
persuading someone to use
your services 136–142
persuasive funnel, the 32–9,
40, 134, 137
when not to use 40
persuasive probing 16–42, 83
positive influencing skills see
influencing others
positively
praise and praising 102,
108–113, 126, 135–6
'principal ploy' in negotiating,
the 59–60
counter-measures against 60
positive influencing see
influencing others
positively
Positive Influencing Skills
courses vii
probing as an influencing tool
16–20, 31, 32, 33, 36–9, 74,
76, 88, 106, 108, 122, 123,
134, 135, 137–142, 145, 147
in depth 25–8, 57
may be unsuccessful 40

probing as a retaliatory form of defence 54, 62
probing as part of negotiating 128–131
probing as part of praising 110, 112
productive meetings *see* meeting, the productive
put-downs 53–4

questions, evaluative 24–5, 41–2
  forced-choice 23–4
  leading 24, 106, 145
  open and/or closed 20, 21–4, 26, 32, 38, 130, 134, 138, 142
  reflective 26–8, 31, 66–8, 69, 106, 108, 115, 130, 138, 139, 142
  to avoid 24–5

rapport 64–82
  subtle 78–82
rapport-breaking 72–8
rapport-building 19, 40, 64–82, 83, 130
reasoning *see* verbal reasoning ability
re-engineering a business *see* business process re-engineering
reflecting technique, the *see* questions, reflective
relationship, building 32, 153
  improving 104
  maintaining 32, 118, 131–2
  your own with yourself 47
repetition, the 'broken record' 117, 118, 122, 123, 131, 135, 138
reprimands 102, 113–118
  positive impact with 116–118

respect as an element in influencing 8–9, 40, 46, 72, 76
response, predictable and/or positive 13, 145
  unpredictable and/or negative 13, 14
  see also fight-or-flight response
retrieval of information *see* information, retrieval
Rogers, Carl 68
rudeness 24, 51

salespersons and sales pitches 39–42, 58–9, 136, 141
selection interview(s) 27, 91–2
self-employment considerations xiii, 136
shy people, a shy person 21, 22–4
signposting what you are about to say 70–72, 86, 88, 106, 120–121, 123, 129, 130, 134, 137, 142, 145, 147
sincerity, body language indications of 99
snooker as an analogue of behaviour viii
space, retention or invasion of our own 96–9
stepping-stone technique for effecting change 150
storage of information *see* information, storage
stress, reduced xiv
stubbornness 45, 133
submissive behaviour 44, 45, 47, 48, 53, 62, 93, 127
suggesting, making suggestions 32, 33–4, 77, 88, 130, 132, 134, 147
  embedded 80–82

on a desired outcome 34, 134
summarising 31, 32, 33, 68, 88, 106, 108, 115, 130, 138, 139, 145, 147
support plan(s) 120, 122, 123
sympathy-seeking 2, 45, 94

talking at rather than talking to 13
talking ratios 20–21
team leadership xii, 43
teamworking and teamworking skills xiii, 43
think, causing someone to 9, 16, 41–2, 77, 106, 108
thinking assertively 46–53, 62
thinking-time in which to marshal thoughts 17–18, 57
threat delivered unthreateningly 51–2, 118, 124
three-part sentence, the 49–50, 55
time management 7, 146
'time travel' as a conversational handicap 20–38
tone of voice as an element in influencing 94, 100, 106, 112, 117, 118, 121, 131
the effects of anger/nervousness on 94, 117
total quality considerations xii

trading during negotiation *see* negotiating skills, trading
transmission of communication 30–32
integration and decoding of 30–31, 32
media for 30
reception of 30
triggering a response 12–13, 14, 17, 77, 145
TSR (That Sounds Reasonable) test ix, x, 15, 153
TV and radio as models of bad practice 25

unhelpfulness 2, 88
understanding others 34, 46, 49, 86, 87, 106
in order that they should understand you 34, 134

verbal reasoning ability, the 44
visualise, causing someone to 16, 34, 139–140
voice, tone of *see* tone of voice as an element in influencing

workforce, involvement/commitment of xii

zones within our own personal space *see* space, retention or invasion of our own

With nearly 100,000 members, the **Institute of Personnel and Development** is the largest organisation in Europe dealing with the management and development of people. The IPD operates its own publishing unit, producing books and research reports for human resource practitioners, students, and general managers charged with people management responsibilities.

Currently there are over 150 titles, covering the full range of personnel and development issues. The books have been commissioned from leading experts in the field and are packed with the latest information and guidance to best practice.

For free copies of the IPD Books Catalogue, please contact the publishing department:

Tel.: 020-8263 3387
Fax: 020-8263 3850
E-mail: publish@ipd.co.uk
Web: www.ipd.co.uk

Orders for books should be sent direct to:

Plymbridge Distributors
Estover
Plymouth
Devon
PL6 7PZ

Credit card orders:
Tel.: 01752 202 301
Fax: 01752 202 333